Biting the Hand That Feeds Me

BITING THE HAND THAT FEEDS ME

Days of Binging, Purging and Recovery

LISA MESSINGER

ARENA PRESS
NOVATO, CALIFORNIA

Editor: David Cole
Typesetting: Pamela Nye
Paste-up: Carol A. McCabe
Cover Design: Naomi Schiff

This book was set in Garamond No. 2

Published by Arena Press, a division of Academic Therapy Publications
20 Commercial Boulevard
Novato, CA 94947-6191

Printed in the United States of America

"I Was A Teenage Fresca Freak" by Lisa Messinger used with per-
mission of *Big Beautiful Woman Magazine.*
Excerpt from *The Journal of Sylvia Plath,* edited by Ted Hughes.
Copyright © 1982 by Ted Hughes as executor of the estate of Sylvia
Plath. Reprinted by permission of Doubleday & Company, Inc.

Library of Congress Cataloging in Publication Data

Messinger, Lisa, 1962-
  Biting the hand that feeds me.

  1. Messinger, Lisa, 1962-   —Health. 2. Messinger,
Lisa, 1962-   —Diaries. 3. Bulimarexia—Patients—
California—Diaries. I. Title.
RC552.M84M47   1986   616.85'2   86-1153
ISBN 0-87879-525-1 (pbk.)

86 87 88 89 90 10 9 8 7 6 5 4 3 2 1

This book is dedicated with love to my mother, the one who was always there, no matter what, no matter when. And to my father, for caring enough to learn to understand.

Table of Contents

"How can I tell them that my happiness streams from having wrenched a piece out of my life, a piece of hurt and beauty, and transformed it to typewritten words on paper? How can [they] know I am justifying my life, my keen emotion, my feeling, by turning it into print?"

Sylvia Plath

Preface

Recently, I gave a lecture to a group of college counseling center psychologists on anorexia nervosa and bulimia, two of the more extreme eating disorders. At the end of the lecture many of the women clinicians privately informed me that although they would not consider themselves to be diagnosable bulimics, they nevertheless perceived themselves as representing variations on the theme. All admitted to being self-conscious about their figures, often attempting last-minute dieting before a weekend party only to overeat and begin a cycle of restrictive food intake afterwards. These women are bright, educated, successful and attractive, and yet preoccupied with self-reproach when they deviated from their diets. They were all well aware of the anatomical and emotional hazards of this chaotic dietary syndrome, but were unable to free themselves from the notion that one is not truly worthwhile if one does not have a slender body.

How can a young high school or college age woman wrench herself free of the compelling need to define her self-worth in terms of her body if her mature counterparts are also caught in the same grip? Can those of us who have gained some perspective on the value of the perfect silhouette in the greater scheme of things assist young girls in recognizing this beauty trap? Perhaps only if we are aware of how most girls are raised with the belief that, despite considerable academic or athletic accomplishments, a female's appearance remains the critical factor in determining her true value in society.

Nowhere has this been so poignantly expressed as in Lisa

Messinger's diary. The reader agonizes with Lisa in page after page of calorie calculations, diet and exercise regimens, body measurement charts and the ever present spector of failure as need gives in to binges followed by remorse and self-recrimination. More importantly, this journal recounts the inner struggle of an individual coming to terms with womanhood. She ultimately rejects the rigid rules of perfection as she painfully absorbs the realities of her life, that her efforts to control and regulate her every move cannot combat the ambiguities and injustices that exist in her world. To attempt perfection is to set oneself up for failure, to never be free of unrealistic and inhuman standards of living.

Lisa's story is told against the backdrop of a "good" girl's middle class upbringing in an environment with which many young women can identify. Lisa's relationship to food initially represents a form of intimacy, one which later in her journal will be supplanted by sexual intimacy, and, finally, by an unconditional caring for herself. Ultimately, Lisa teaches herself that her body will not betray her if she trusts her basic feelings and judges that her hunger for love and recognition can never be filled by food. As Lisa abandons rigid, dichotomous thinking she learns to accept new ways of nourishing her spirit.

The value of Lisa's diary for young women derives, first, from the bleak fact that bulimia and anorexia nervosa have reached epidemic proportions in this nation, with researchers estimating anywhere from ten to thirty-five percent of all women between the ages of fourteen and thirty-five as victims. College age women especially continue to endure the punishing effects of self-starvation and binge eating while nurturing the idea that there is only one acceptable body type, and life is not worth living without it.

Second, Lisa's struggle to overcome her eating disorder is not a fairy tale success story: her battle is checkered with defeats and setbacks, and her ultimate victory is not in attaining a magic number on the bathroom scale, but in accepting her body as nature probably intended it, with food serving a neutral role, merely as a means to replenish nutrients, and not as an intimidating foe.

Finally, Lisa's story helps professionals, parents and her contemporaries to understand how an addiction can permeate the lifestyle of a well-meaning adolescent who attempted to apply perfectionistic standards to every aspect of her being in hope that she would be loved and approved of by her family and her peers. It would seem that the prevention of these insidious eating disorders could be aided by encouraging high school and college students to read this book and understand that the key to self-acceptance and fulfillment has little to do with one's body measurements.

As a practicing psychologist with a specialty in eating disorders, I can appreciate the agony of Lisa's plight. As her former therapist, I can respect the dedication and commitment to recovery that appears on every page of her diary. Lisa's journey to self-discovery is one that can be realized by every sufferer of eating disorders with patience, professional support, and a willingness to alter one's belief in rigid, self-destructive patterns of behavior.

Anita B. Siegman, Ph.D.
Los Angeles, California
October, 1985

Introduction

There always used to be a few candy wrappers under my bed. Not candy *bar* wrappers, but candy *bag* wrappers. I used to eat bags of candy, bags of cookies, bags of junk food, cartons of ice cream, dozens of doughnuts and entire cakes. I wasn't fat. I wasn't hungry. I wasn't even a food-lover. I hated most of the food I ate almost as much as I hated myself. I was a bulimic.

Actually, I was more fortunate than most bulimics. I didn't resort to vomiting. Nevertheless, I fell within the ever widening spectrum of people with serious eating problems, people with unreasonable, life-consuming concerns regarding body and weight and eating. My form of purging may not have been vomiting, but nevertheless it was a "purge," a way to "purify" myself. It was a way to rid myself of the guilt I felt over eating. I was caught in an addictive cycle of binging, followed by starvation dieting and compulsive exercising—not occasionally, but every day. I was a slave to a scale and a twisted set of self-imposed rules.

It's hard to remember those rules. I did, however, write most of them down in my diary. The front cover read "One Year Diary," next to which I wrote, "You wanna make a bet!" I wrote sporadically in that diary for over six years, from the ages of fifteen through twenty-two. It tells my story. Perhaps it tells yours, too, or one like it. Because we who are entangled in self-destructive, energy-consuming cycles are not alone.

In 1981, my psychologist, Francine Snyder, asked if she could include some of my writing in a book she was putting together about bulimia. There was my diary, a few journals, a lot of assorted papers, and a couple of scrapbooks. As I read over them I realized that, without trying, I had caught on paper an obsession, a compulsion. I had written about it almost at its birth, before I even knew what it was, right through the recovery I was starting to experience in 1981.

People afflicted with an eating disorder are often secretive and find few outlets for their real feelings. Writing for me was partly this, but it was also more. I always wanted to be a writer. And I always wrote even when I didn't know I wanted to be a writer. While I was in college, I had my first professional submission accepted by a national magazine. *Big Beautiful Woman* then asked me, a just-turning twenty year old, to be a contributing reporter, which I was for a good part of a year. I went on to get my degree in journalism and women's studies from the University of Southern California and I am now a regular contributing reporter and city correspondent for a mid-circulation newspaper in Southern California, a free lance writer, and a frequent columnist for the Los Angeles National Organization for Women newspaper.

I say this in order to provide some perspective on why I thought my diary might speak to a broad audience. I may have been suffering with the trauma of an eating disorder through most of the years this book covers (1977-1984); however, I was always a writer. The book that follows was never merely "Dear Diary." Although I never expected anyone else to read it, I was always, for some reason, addressing my thoughts "Dear World."

As it developed over the years, however, this work seemed to transcend the realm of an eating disorder book, and that is why I am most proud of it.

Because this book is based on my real life, I have changed most of the character names, physical descriptions and other details regarding peoples lives. Virtually all of this was written as it happened. I have added just a few words here and there if something needed clarification.

I would like to thank each and every person who helped me and touched me over the years. A project spanning time like this makes one realize how fleeting and yet truly important relationships are.

It also makes one realize that although we may be blessed with the love of a lover, of friends or family, no matter how close, we each ultimately travel alone. We can only hope to make our lives as satisfy ing and ultimately valid as we can. I am grateful, at such a young age for the opportunity to contribute to the literature on eating disorders and issues affecting womens' lives.

Lisa Messinger
November 1985

1. Adolescence

FEBRUARY 9, 1977

"Tomorrow is the first day of the rest of my life!" I'm turning over a new leaf. I will no longer be shy. I will be confident. I will be able to talk with boys with ease. I won't wonder if I look good. I will look good.

The biggest thing on my mind is the math test. I'll try my best. (I hope I do good! Real good!!) I guess I'm afraid of not doing well. I feel like everyone expects so much of me, including me.

I'm going to act the way I used to with Sam, insults and all. I still want him to be my friend. I guess I'm just jealous. I hate hearing boys like Sam talking about other girls. What's wrong with me? They treat me as though I were nothing but a huge brain! I hate being classified as that! Just because I get all A's doesn't mean I'm not a normal girl.

Shelly's "interested look" is driving me crazy! I guess it's bothering me because I was jealous when they said how good at tennis she was.

Today, I have to say, I was really flabbergasted. At lunch, Staci very bluntly informed me that she'd appreciate it if I'd stop spreading rumors about her! Well, I had no idea what she was talking about. She went on muttering that I said that she got a C on a test and that I would have cried if it had been me. I knew what she meant. I had told Cindy something similar (not word for word) to that about two weeks ago. There was nothing wrong with me telling my best friend how I felt about someone! Cindy told Staci something I had told her in private. I felt like crying. I'm going to call Cindy and talk this out. I'm sure, since she was sitting right there, she knows I'm upset with her. Something else bothered me. All my friends (?) just sat there as Staci preached my wrongdoings. It was as if they had already heard the story.

Well, I got a B+ on my world studies test. I think one question away from an A. I was disappointed, but recovered. Got an A on my Spanish test. Hallelujah! I thought I might never see another one. Thought I was slipping. I guess I've finally got my footing again!

MARCH 20, 1977

Why can't I giggle? Why can't I sit around at lunch and giggle and talk about boys? Why do I have to go to the library and study? Why do I feel mortified sitting around with a bunch of giggling girls?

I don't know what to do. If I leave them, these friends from junior high school and even elementary school, I will have no one. But having no one is beginning to seem more and more preferable.

I couldn't believe it when they started cutting Sam down right in front of me. They know what good friends we are. And they're just jealous. Sam's on the baseball team and the honor roll, and what do they have, nothing! Forget it, I think I'll just take Sam and take my chances and just move on. Forget this. We are so different.

JULY 1, 1977

Sam's my boyfriend! Jim Michaels called! Mike Gold called last week. Well, I've done it! I'm at ease with boys and not so unpopular either! I guess I'm proud. Sam says he's in love with me. I'm skeptical. We've been joking friends for so long, I couldn't believe it when he kissed me and told me he loved me. I *know* I'm not in love with anyone now! I really do like him though, and I like kissing, too. That surprises me, but I'm curious to find out what comes next. Although I almost slammed the door in his face when he tried more than the tiniest little kiss. Well, I hope Jim Stern isn't getting any ideas, because I'm not. Sam. Sam. Sam.

Well, I still hope to grow.

P.S. I've escaped from those idiotic, immature friends, who were not really friends at all.

West Valley High School
Abuela School District

March 15, 1977

Miss Lisa Messinger
7089 Cardinal Drive
Woodland Hills, California

Dear Lisa:

Well, you did it again! Another perfect semester! I'm really
impressed with your academic achievement and can assure you, as
a result, you will reap many fine rewards. The really neat part
is that in addition to the perfect grades, you found time to
participate in our drama program thus disproving the "Book Worm
Theory".

Maintaining a 4.0 grade point average is not an easy task and
I commend you for your accomplishment. Most people fail to realize
the effort that is necessary to achieve this level of scholarship.
It takes motivation, dedication, and above all, hard work. You
have apparently set high goals for yourself and have demonstrated
the willingness to give high priority to them. Your parents must
be very proud and pleased with your success and I am sure they
also deserve a pat on the back.

Enclosed you will find your well-earned "Outstanding 'A' Student
Pass".

The future should hold many interesting experiences for you and
I am looking forward to the opportunity of guiding you through
the remainder of your high school years.

Sincerely,

Albert E. Acton
Principal

/m

JULY 2, 1977

At first it's just jokes, insults too,
You're sure that he despises you.
Then he calls for an assignment, says everyone else is out.
"You've been on the phone for two hours!" you hear your mother
shout.
You never knew you could find so much to talk about.

Back at school, you're closer than ever.
But as to being more than friends, never.
You can talk about anything and everything.
Why is it you nearly jump every time you hear the phone ring?
You feel close, true, but it lacks that special "zing."

The last day of school is finally here.
In his eyes, could it be a trace of fear?
The yearbooks are signed, and you see you haven't passed the joking
stage.
But, still, you search for a hidden message on the page.
The play's over. We were actors, the classroom our stage.

But, wait! He walks you home, there's a kiss, and nothing will ever,
can ever, be the same.

AUGUST 1, 1977

Well, we just drifted apart. Phooey! I go to Hawaii for two weeks with
Mom and Dad and Robert and we never see see each other again.
That really makes a lot of sense!

Sam is immature. He tells me he loves me, and then I go to Hawaii
for my brother's bar mitzvah gift and he never calls again. I can't call
him. I used to be able to when it was for homework or something.
Not about this.

I don't even care. This was not working out, these two weeks of
him telling me that when we're sixteen he'll get away from his drinking mother and we'll get married.

I'm not going anywhere when I'm sixteen. Besides, I don't even
like kissing him, the little that I did.

There's got to be a lot more to see than this.

NOVEMBER 10, 1977

I'm on the verge of a new beginning. I can feel it! Get this, now I'm the one starting the conversations with boys. Mark Jefferson saying how cute I am. It's the first time I may not get A's. I may get a B+ in algebra II (maybe an A−). Me and Sam, we're always continuing. Things were very awkward after our stormy, not to mention short, romance. But *I* broke the ice. I called him on Halloween (for help in math, ha-ha.) We're friends like always again. Relief. To be more than friends is just too complicated. He is, though, an extremely special person.

Things are really going well. My sweet sixteen party!!! Rob Jeffries a possible guest. Wow! One boyfriend . . . not for me, today anyway. I'm happy. I'm actually confident. I have a feeling that things will get even better, too. I really felt strongly about Mike. Then, all of a sudden I changed my mind. Well, from now on it's me, me, me. I keep thinking about what was with Sam and me. What does that mean, Doctor?

Terri, Kim (a new friend I really like), Amy. They're a new group. They're smart, they play tennis, they're nice, and they'll do for now. I still want to grow with boys and girls.

JANUARY 21, 1978

The real me is a pretty, smart, attractive and even sexy girl. The me that shows is insecure, aloof and inferior feeling. Why? And, can I change?

JANUARY 27, 1978

Happiness isn't the word. I don't know what the word is, but I feel good about me! Sixteen years old and I gave a sweet sixteen party (never thought I could). It really did go pretty well. Kim. Finally a friend that seems just right for me. Mike. I can't believe it, I asked him to the Sadie Hawkins' Dance. I just hope it all works out. Nothing really special yet, but I do like him a lot. Sam. Still in the picture, I really care about him. I can't pinpoint the feeling, talk about confusing! Rob. A hope for the future. I'm not that taken with him, even though he's beautiful and gorgeous and smart. I guess that proves something. I'm looking, waiting, for true love. It still seems a long way off.

A's. I got them. It really is important.

I told Sam how I felt about his teasing me all the time. It felt good.

Lilli. I have to admit I was jealous. Why? I don't know, way inside.

Lucky I'm never really unhappy. But right now I'm happy not because of one specific thing, just because I'm me.

FEBRUARY 14, 1978

Dear Louise,

It's been awhile, how are you? I can't stand this weather.

February 24 is the school's first semi-formal Sadie Hawkins' dance, I got my courage up and asked (guess who?), remember Mike? Well, that's who I asked. He said that he'd love to. I got an outfit yesterday, a light blue satin jumpsuit. I think we might do something before or after.

Louise, I really wish you were here instead of all the way in Antelope Valley. I know it's only an hour and a half away, but still! So much has been happening, and while my mom tries to understand she's got her own ideas. Make sure nobody reads this. Write back soon. Maybe you can give me some advice.

Remember Sam? Well, he compared us again. He told me I should wear a lower, more suggestive shirt, he said that's what boys like. When he saw I wasn't paying attention, he said, "You're no fun. Your cousin Louise is fun, she doesn't act disgusted to hear stuff like you, you just act like you hate it."

And then the other day right in math, Sam starts telling me what a "good girl" I am, never did a thing wrong in my life. Then he says he can't wait to see me after I "lose my virginity." He said it'll probably be when I'm 35 and married. Then he said, "Who knows? It might be Mike!" I was getting mad. He said that now that I was 16 I was desperate for sex, and that's why *I* was going after Mike (ha-ha). Then he said he wanted to give me some advice about taking Mike to the dance. I told him to shut up, so he wrote me a note saying that all Mike wants is sex, and that I better give it to him or he won't go. You know, I've been called "sweet" and "saint" and "perfect" a lot these past weeks. If you act like you like a boy, does that mean he'll think you want him to try something?

We had carnations for sale for Valentine's Day. I sent one to Mike Gold, who I really do like and probably should have asked to the Sadie Hawkins' dance. I also sent one to Rod Burke (his brother told my brother that he's madly in love with me), also to Jim Stern, and, you won't believe it, to Sam (before he gave me his sex education lecture).

I ran my jog-a-thon, 18 laps in an hour. Not that fantastic, but it was fun.

So, what's new in your always exciting life? How's Craig? Is he still going for Heather or has he realized that you're the one for him? Well, I hope you can come and stay over Easter. Please write back soon, especially what you think of all this with Sam and Mike.

Love,
Lisa

FEBRUARY 17, 1978

Dear Louise,

Well, I'm glad you wrote back so fast. How was your Valentine's Day? Discover any secret admirers? The carnations delivered at school turned out to be plants because the flowers got ruined by rain. They were cute—you wrote a little message and the person got it in their class. I didn't think I'd get any, but I got one from Rod (the cute one who I think is so sweet). He just wrote, ''Always, Rod.'' I kinda wish I asked him to the Sadie Hawkins' dance, but anyway, I sent him one too.

I'm really glad that I did ask Mike to the dance. After all, these guys may be cute and on the basketball team, but they're more friends (although I'd go out with them)! But Mike is the one I've thought and thought and thought about. All this time, I mean way back when Sam proclaimed his love for me, it was Mike who I had the crush on. I've never felt this strongly before. It's like I can't control myself. I think about him all the time. He's so charming and smart and CUTE! I decided I'm not wearing the jumpsuit to the dance. It's just too much. I'm going to get something else.

Well, I've got another question for my cousin, the authority. If a guy really likes you a lot and you like him as a good friend and that's it, how would you handle it if he wants you to like him like he likes you? What I'm talking about is Jim Stern, I think I really hurt him. He wants me to go to the basketball party and I say sure. He wants me to go out with him when he gets his car and I say sure. He asks me if I've asked someone to the dance, and I say sure. Not sure, but yes. I could tell he thought I really liked him. I don't see anything wrong with liking lots of guys, do you? Why tie yourself down when you can do lots of things with lots of people? Although, all I really want is for Mike to like me.

My mom's ideas . . . I don't know. I just think that some time I might really want to give/get more than a goodnight kiss. Not much more. What are your thoughts on this?

Write back soon and tell me about you and Craig. I hope everything with Gus works out too! I'll certainly have a lot of news next time about the dance!!!!!!

Love,
Lisa

FEBRUARY 20, 1978

Well, this is the worst day of my life. Period. I feel awful. I cried all night. Not one hour. Not two hours. All night.

I called my mom at her card game. I've never done that. I just couldn't believe it. I was so upset.

I was baking cookies, and he called. He can't go. I bought two outfits, and he can't go. He lied, too. I didn't think so when he called, but now I know.

He said his mom was going out of town and he had to go to his dad's in Orange County. One day before the dance! I said, "Can't you stay with Ken?" "No," he said, "my mom said, no. I promised my dad."

When I got off the phone I couldn't stop crying, and I called my mom.

Then, yesterday, the *day of the dance*, I couldn't believe it. I got my driver's license, passed the test, was driving with my mom for the first time up my street, and who do I see, Sam and Mike! I said to my mom, "That's Sam and Mike, they're walking up to *our* house. Don't look!"

At home I made my brother look out the window, and there they were! They started walking around in my back yard! I went out and said, "You're trespassing." They said they were just going around and bothering everyone they knew named Lisa. They went over to Lisa Spencer's and now me.

I said to Mike, "I thought you were going to your dad's."

"Oh, I didn't have to, or I'm going later," he said.

Then Mike said he was going to walk over to Mark Kaplan's, and

13

Sam begged to use the bathroom. So finally I let him inside. When Mike was gone Sam said, you know why Mike didn't want to go with you? He just didn't want to. He never did. He was never going to go. How could you have thought he'd go with you? You're such a prude. He never liked you, and I never did either. You think I was serious when I said everything to you this summer? That was a whole game with Mike and me to see how far you'd go along.

I said, "That's not true about you. I just hurt you and now you're trying to hurt me by saying all this."

"But," he said, "you'll never really know that, will you? You'll never really know. Ha-ha."

MAY 28, 1978

It's the first time I'm writing without good news. I mean I'm not actually depressed, or am I? Nothing seems right. I'm shaky with everything, boys, friends, even family and me. I know eventually something will happen, but I just don't know when. *I will lose the weight and look and feel terrific.* I gained six pounds. I can't believe it. This has really pushed me over the limit, 126 pounds! God, I can't take this. Now that it's written that I'll lose it, it's set. I think I'll just remember, "We can take forever a minute at a time." My philosophy now. The summer will be nice. Joining the tennis club like everyone else on the team would have been. Oh well, no sense fighting a losing battle. Jim Stern's junior prom seems like a long time ago. Very interesting. I think I must have let out a huge sigh when Jim just hugged me. Maybe I was just a little disappointed. Nah, that's ultra-hypocritical! I guess I really am pretty special. I'll make it!

JULY 7, 1978

Up to this point, I have been writing sporadically. I would like to start putting my feelings on paper more frequently. I'm always fascinated when I look back at the entries, but actually being able to recapture the emotions is hard. I am writing this solely for me. Maybe I'll be able to see myself changing, growing, progressing.

I would like to lose weight and look and feel terrific. The question is, can I? Well, I guess anything's possible. I really do want to, but I'm afraid. I have this strange notion that every single problem I have will disappear with those pounds. What if they don't, or what if I work really hard, and I can't do it and I don't know why. I really have to go back to school as a different person. Last year wasn't the pits. Or was it?? I must do this, if for no one else, for me. I deserve the confidence it will give me.

I want to write about something that I have trouble admitting even to myself. The way I eat is definitely weird! I'm not always sure why I do it. All I know is, *I must stop.* If I don't, what will my future be? When I live alone, it'll be too easy. I'll be a blimp. Do I need help? I really don't think so. I mean, I'm not sick! Well, that's just it, I'm quitting cold turkey. Tonight will be the test, babysitting. Oh, God, when I think back to every Saturday night for years, eating like a pig! The candy, the soda, the cookies, the ice cream, all the things we never had at home. How many times did I eat and eat and eat and then run around the house while the kids slept doing push-ups, sit-ups, jumping jacks, anything to erase the Oreos, the Ding Dongs, the cans of Coke, the TV dinners? How many times did I stare at myself in the bathroom mirror wondering how many pounds I had gained, anxious for tomorrow when I could start fresh and, hopefully, not eat at all.

I'm fed up with myself! Why am I starting to cry? Because it's true, I want to change. I guess I *can* do anything! Well, I can't go on like this. I hate myself when I do it. I hate myself! I want to like myself. *I will.*

I felt really, really depressed and sad on my year anniversary with Sam, my first boyfriend. I don't know why. I remembered everything. Everything about Sam, and about Sam and Mike came flooding back.

Talking to Krista Jennings at the barbecue on Saturday I realized that even though I'm as straight as the shortest distance between two points (straighter), I wouldn't want to be like her for anything. I wonder a lot if I'm normal. I can't stand the taste of alcohol, even wine. I know I never will. I've never had even one drink in my entire life. I'm not at all curious to even try marijuana, or any drugs, or smoking—even once.

Some world, you have to wonder if it's abnormal to be a totally logical thinking, sensible, healthy, sane, sober, intelligent person.

Well, I'll keep you updated on my progress, and anytime I feel weak, I'll write instead of eat.

JULY 8, 1978

OFFICIAL CONTRACT

I, Lisa Dale Messinger, do hereby swear never to binge again. *Never.* I realize that this is in my best interest, and my best interest *is* my

best interest!
I love *me!*

Signed,
Lisa Dale Messinger

JULY 10, 1978

Nobody's awake, but I've had a revelation! All I have to do to weigh 115 by August 31 is to lose a quarter of a pound a day! I can do that! That's one pound every four days. Maybe, if I'm good, I can even lose more! This really gives me confidence! Even if I have, by cheating spells, gone up to 128, I can still lose 13 pounds in 52 days. Isn't that great! It makes it seem so much more attainable. Wow. I guess this is positive thinking!

JULY 18, 1978

MEAL TICKET EXCHANGES
(According to my nutritionist)

Breakfast:
    1 cup nonfat milk
    1 fruit
    1 bread
    1 meat (optional)
    1 tsp. fat

Lunch:
    vegetables (free)
    1 fruit
    1 bread
    2 meats
    1 tsp. fat

Snack:
    (two out of three)
    1 fruit
    1 bread
    1 meat

Dinner:
    1 cup nonfat milk
    vegetables (free)
    1 fruit
    1 bread
    3 meats
    1 tsp. fat

JULY 31, 1978

I am so *proud!* It's 1:26A.M. I can't sleep so I'm trying on clothes. Guess who just zipped up those previously given up on white gauchos, and guess who doesn't look that shabby in her size five satin jump suit that didn't fit six months ago? Hallelujah!

Two weeks with my nutritionist and I don't believe it. Slowly but *surely* I'm disappearing. I'm so glad mom told me about her friend who was seeing this nutritionist and asked if I would want to go. It's the *real me* that's beginning to appear!

Keep up the good work!

SEPTEMBER 23, 1978

Could it be magic? Right now, I'm really not sure. You'll be one of the first to know if it is. Chris seems fantastic to me, but looks and personality aren't everything. Well, I shouldn't get my hopes up, Ellen did meet him first and does have two classes with him. I'll just have to play it by ear. I wish . . . well, I'm surviving better than ever before. I've got more friends now and am happy, with or without Mr. Right!

By seeing the nutritionist this summer (and still going), at this, the start of my junior year, I've lost at least 14½ pounds. I weigh about 116. People say I really look thin. I still need a little convincing. If this situation with Chris works out I'll be shocked.

NOVEMBER 17, 1978

I, Lisa Messinger, will weigh 115 pounds.

I, Lisa Messinger, will accomplish this by December 4, 1978.

I, Lisa Messinger, do swear, on my honor, to eat sensibly from this day forward.

After each "balanced" meal a penny will be put in a jar.

My reward upon completion will be—assuming that said weight has been maintained for three weeks, until 25, December, 1978 (during this period every "balanced" meal will warrant a nickel)—a $150.00 wardrobe.

I do hereby swear that I comprehend and will uphold the terms laid out in this contract.

Officially,
Lisa Messinger

TRENT BROADCASTING COMPANY
5th Avenue
New York, NY

November 30, 1978

Lisa Messinger
7089 Cardinal Drive
Woodland Hills, CA 91365

Dear Lisa,

As a producer for "K.I.D. NETWORK" I've received a letter from
you stating that you would like to appear as a news reporter
on our show.

To be a reporter for "K.I.D. NETWORK," you have to send us
a letter with an idea for a story from your neighborhood that
we would be able to film with you as a correspondent. This
story idea should appeal to kids all over the country. If we
like the idea, we'll talk to you about it.

If you want to write us back with an idea, please include
a picture of yourself. Please also let us know your age and
telephone number.

Thanks from the "K.I.D. NETWORK."

Sincerely,

Jerry Dawber

Jerry Dawber
Executive Producer

DECEMBER 31, 1978

NEW YEAR'S RESOLUTIONS

Think positive thoughts about myself.
Keep weight and figure at a point where I am happy about myself.
Be happy.
Be neater.
Be confident.
I Lisa Messinger do hereby swear to uphold these vows.

Signed sincerely,
Lisa Messinger

JANUARY 21, 1979

Well, it's the last day of my sixteenth year. I'm looking forward to getting older, being able to do more things and meet more people. Right now I'm very close to Cheri and (good friends, too, with) her boyfriend Mike. *I wish I had a boyfriend.* I know the mature attitude is just to wait for "my time to come." But I can't help wondering what it would be like to love someone, or at least really like them a lot and feel comfortable with them. I would not count Allan as a boyfriend (although he'd probably disagree). Just because we go out a lot doesn't mean we're a couple. He's nice and he's smart and he wants to be a reporter, but that's it. I don't want anything more with him.

Maybe I'm searching for something that doesn't exist. Oh, well. I still lack confidence in myself. I start building it up tomorrow!

I'm all right, I suppose.

FEBRUARY 13, 1979

Wish me luck. Tomorrow is Valentine's Day, and I am going to follow my heart. I have a good feeling inside that I've finally found someone who's good for me. Shyness on both parts, however, can definitely be a deterrent.

Even though Mike and Cheri are both very nice, apart and together, what they have would not be right for me. It's too intense. Maybe I'm on the brink of a relationship. Maybe not. Perry certainly is handsome. He certainly is. There's not much doubt there. *Very* intelligent too. So logical. And thinks like I do about so much. So easy to talk to, that is, when we have a real opportunity to talk. My feelings are right. I know it. This time it's special. Tomorrow my life might change. That's exciting. I'm not used to making a move like this. Although, I guess most people wouldn't consider giving a boy a valentine card such a big move. It's just that it's such a special recipient!

Keep that nerve up!

P.M. So I didn't have the nerve. What else is new?

FEBRUARY 17, 1979

Connie Chung
Steve Edwards
Two on the Town
KNXT

Dear Ms. Chung & Mr. Edwards:

My reasons for writing are two-fold. First, I am seventeen years old and intent on becoming a broadcast journalist. I have taken broad-casting classes in school and have gotten experience on the local level. However, the real catalyst to my decision was the day I spent as reporter Pete Pepper's "shadow" for the Channel 2 newscast taping. After seeing the two of you and the rest of the newsteam at work, I was hooked. This brings me to my first question: Why aren't teens represented on TV? Although shows like *30 Minutes* and *Kids Are People Too* are directed toward young people, they are hosted by adults. Teenagers are apparent in other areas, from idolized actors to imprisoned criminals.

I would like to help break this barrier by appearing on *Two on the Town* as one of the weekly guest hosts you advertised for on TV. My story idea deals with a serious, tragic and, too often, fatal issue that affects teens, adults and society as well, teenage suicide. I am on the speech team at my school (last year I was a National Forensic League State Finalist) and my current oratory deals with this topic. Through my research and interviews, I have become deeply concerned. Like most people, I was unaware of the great depth of this problem. Consider these statistics. Every year, 6000 teens commit suicide, and as many as 600,000 attempt it. The adolescent suicide rate has risen almost 300% in just twenty years. Suicide is now the second leading cause of death among teens. Nearly 50% of all teenagers think about suicide, and almost 20% attempt it, one in five! Why? What can we do about it? Many experts believe a broad educational effort is needed, that schools and suicide prevention centers should be combined in an effort to squelch the ''epidemic.''

My expose could be filmed at a suicide prevention center. An opening would explain the gravity of the problem. I could then interview a teen who has attempted suicide, and a suicide expert who could give possible explanations and solutions.

Teen suicide is still a taboo subject. Only when we eliminate the myths can the problem be dealt with effectively.

Two on the Town can help to inform the public, and, at the same time, give a future broadcaster her first break!

> Thank you,
> *Lisa Messinger*

FEBRUARY 23, 1979

Dennis Swanson
News Director
KABC Eyewitness News

Dear Dr. Swanson:

Thank you for responding so quickly to my previous letter. I was very excited to learn that you had considered the idea of a teenage reporter, and would take the time to view my audition tape. It all goes to show that your openmindedness and philosophy of there being more to life than news, weather, and sports is more than just talk. My response has been delayed because I have had trouble obtaining my original tape. During this interval, I have made an additional tape. I would greatly appreciate it if I could enhance my presentation with a personal meeting.

Becoming a broadcast journalist is my dream. As Helen Keller once said, ''Follow your dreams, for as you dream you shall become.''

Thank you very much for reading my letters and for taking a sincere interest in the concerns of your viewers.

> Thank you,
> *Lisa Messinger*

MARCH 12, 1979

I am very displeased with myself. I am fat! I am fat! I am fat! I hate myself! Maybe I'm not really fat, but if that's how I feel, then there's really not much difference. I must change. I know I've said it before. I do not want to be as fat as I was last summer. One hundred thirty pounds. No way. With each pound it'll be harder!

If I begin now (and I know how to do it, too, because of going to the nutritionist last summer) then by this summer, I should be all set! If I could like myself in a bathing suit that would be real progress! I must begin to feel more secure.

I suppose I'm like clay. I can leave myself in a blob or mold myself into a work of art.

MARCH 22, 1979

Spring will bring the turning over of a new leaf and a new life.

APRIL 3, 1979

Dear Congressman Goldwater:

I have long had a dream of the ideal way to spend the summer following my high school graduation (summer 1980). I would greatly appreciate your help in making my dream a reality. I would consider it a privilege and an invaluable experience to have the opportunity to serve as a page in Congress. I understand the necessary qualifications, academic prowess, favorable recommendations, and corresponding interests. I feel that I fulfill these requirements. I have maintained a 4.0 grade average and am ranked first in my class. I was valedictorian at my junior high school graduation. I am extremely interested in politics, and am seriously considering the field as a future endeavor. My other possible career goals include broadcast journalism and law. My interests are related to these fields. As a freshman, I was editor-in-chief of our school newspaper. Incidentally, one of the highlights of my year as editor was an interview with you! In addition, I have been a member of the forensic and debate team for the past three years. During this time I have participated in a number of student congresses. In these the speakers play the part of congressmen attempting to pass legislation. I have learned a great deal through these experiences and I would love to have the chance to observe the real life model of our enactments. I have greatly enjoyed these speech experiences and was proud to be one of the first three students to represent our high school at the State Forensics Finals in San Diego earlier this month. I have been reading about the duties and life style of a Congressional page, and the more I learn the more enthusiastic I become. I have included applicable recommendations and would gladly furnish any other necessary information.

I would consider it a privilege to speak or meet with you in the future.

Thank You,
Lisa Messinger

(Never Sent)

JUNE 28, 1979

I have to take this hostessing job. It will help me. You can't be shy when your job is to help people, to smile, to chat, to direct to a table. I'll have to do it. It'll be my job.

And in the more real world I'll just be me. No grades. Just me. If I'm pretty, I'm pretty. If I'm smart, I'm smart.

This will help me become not shy, which I know I must become.

JULY 18, 1979

Wow. Did I expect this? This is okay. Here I am out in the real world, and I'm finally being noticed a little bit. My favorite, (twenty-eight), sits at the counter and asks me out on dates! And he's not the only one who says things.

Maybe my parents have been right, maybe I am pretty. From what they say these guys sem to think so, too, and I weigh 120.

CBS
NEWS

A Division of CBS Inc.
524 West 57 Street
New York, New York 10019
(212)975-4321

March 22, 1979

Dear Ms. Messinger:

Thank you for your interest in 30 MINUTES. I think you summed
it up when you said that Christopher Glenn and Betsy Aaron are
serious journalists. Indeed they are with considerable experience
behind them. That was our first consideration in selecting the
hosts for this broadcast. I'd like to be able to give you a
chance but before you could be considered you would have had to
already shown the type of journalism background and talent which
is the hallmark of CBS News.

Good luck.

Yours truly,

Joel Heller
Executive Producer
30 MINUTES

Ms. Lisa Messinger
7089 Cardinal Drive
Woodland Hills, CA 91365

JULY 20, 1979

Confusion

I think . . .
I know that I think . . .
I think that I know . . .
I think that I know what I think . . .
I know what I know . . .
I think?

AUGUST 1, 1979

What are you doing? List it, then maybe you'll see:

strawberry shortcake	chocolate sauce
cream of potato soup	cheddar cheese soup
chocolate pudding	cream of chicken soup

You're supposed to be the take-out girl. Stop taking out to the bathroom or home! Stop it!

AUGUST 20, 1979

Well, I hope I'm not jumping the gun again! I've thought so many times that something was going to happen between us and I've been wrong, and we've just stayed friends. I really feel like this time it could be different though. I get a funny feeling in my stomach. Could it be love? No, now you are jumping ahead. Take your time. Don't blow it! Will Perry call? He will. He said so! I know he likes me. I just know it. You don't talk like that to someone you don't like. But how much? I wonder what's going to happen. I guess I have to make it happen.

Well, I feel good and that's good. 120 pounds is a nice round number. Pardon, a nice slim number, and still losing. I won't blow that again. So am I pretty? Sometimes I think so. Sometimes not. Enough people say so. Why always the *wrong* people?

Well, Perry's call just came and so did more doubts. Everything I just said about us might be void. Might be!

SEPTEMBER 1, 1979

Perry

   This is a message that comes with the hope that you will *finally* get the message! You're so smart and quick-minded that it's really very surprising that it takes you so long to figure out such a simple little thing. Or maybe you have already figured it out? I know this is resorting to a pretty juvenile, junior-highish mode of communication, but I don't know what else to do. If you would just cooperate, it would all be so simple! Now here's my plan. (You have a relatively easy part.) Just come to me and say, "I have something I want to tell you." Then I'll say, "Don't say another word. I understand." Eight little words that have a big meaning. Oh, what's the point? I'll never have the nerve. As if I ever did!

2. Senior Year

SEPTEMBER 19, 1979

Bust: 35''

Waist: 27¼''

Hips: 37''

Midriff: 35¼''

Upper arm: 13''

Upper leg: 23''

Lower leg: 12½''

Calf: 8''

Lower arm: 8¼''

OCTOBER 18, 1979

Almost eighteen. Almost an adult. Almost grown-up. Almost out on
my own. "Almost" seems to be the story of my life. I feel kind of
out of it this year. You know, the awkward year. The in-between one.
I keep wondering where I'll be and what I'll be doing next year. If I
had to guess (and wish), I'd say I'll be at UCLA living in the dorm.
I'd be surprised if I were in an apartment or at home, and even more
surprised if I were at another school.

This year I just can't get into anything, my classes, the tennis team
or the speech team. My interest level seems to have disappeared.
That's about the state of my love life too, non-existent. Sometimes I
wonder if there are any other normal acting, intelligent people who are
as inexperienced in the field of sex as I am. With things like smoking
and drugs I have absolutely no interest. Drinking I just plain dislike.

But sex, if I found the right person I would like to try. Maybe not the whole banana, but I'd certainly like to get a little experience behind me.

Well, I did one good thing. I joined a health club. I wonder if by next year it will have paid off?

Oh, Prince Charming, come out, come out wherever you are! Or at least send one of your friends to keep me occupied until you get here.

Perry, I just give up. Not that I tried all that hard. But you're much too shy (I hope), and I can't, no matter how much I think about it, make that first move.

It just seems like nothing very important is happening to me. Or maybe I just don't notice it. Maybe this is life.

OCTOBER 22, 1979

Happy birthday to me! Happy birthday to me! Oh, I know I'm exactly three months off. But I've already decided to present to myself, a new me, and I've got three whole months to deliver. It won't stop there, and I won't sluff off in the meantime. I am in the process of creating a more beautiful me through proper nutrition and exercise. Oh, I can just imagine me three months from now.

Maybe I can even do it before. At any rate, it *will* happen, and afterward it will be my way of life!!

OCTOBER 30, 1979

There's, of course, going to be no way I'm going to go to UCLA now. They don't even have a journalism major there, let alone a broadcast journalism major.

No, I have seen my school. Thank God I competed in a speech tournament there. USC. "The ghetto," my mother always said. What a picture I had of it in my mind. Ha! This school is beautiful.

Somehow I know that when I look in the counseling center's college catalogs next week, I will find a broadcast journalism major at USC. At my school.

NOVEMBER 13, 1979

Day One
of thirty days spent following Overeater's Anonymous diet with an O.A. sponsor

Breakfast:	Lunch:
1 egg	4 oz. tuna fish
1 oz. cheddar cheese	1 serving cooked carrots
1 apple	finger salad with lettuce
tea with artificial sweetener	(Make sure it's all right to have
	lettuce in a finger salad.)
	diet soda

Dinner:
4 oz. turkey without skin
1 serving string beans
2 cups salad with diet dressing
diet soda

NOVEMBER 15, 1979

Finally, I have met people I can talk to at Overeater's Anonymous.

Go at night, spill out your guts, come home and lie again. Keep the truth hidden.

The strongest feeling I had at OA, though, was fear and shock. Older people, like in their 40s or 60s, were talking about the same compulsive eating problems that I have.

Somehow I always imagined that this ended. I never pictured having this in college or, especially, in later life. I'm going to have a tremendously successful career and life and marriage. I never pictured this. I always thought that it would just go away when I got out of high school.

Well, now I'm scared to death and more determined to get out of this thing soon, because I see in her eyes and hers and hers and his and his and hers that it doesn't just end. I can't waste my life, not *my* life.

DECEMBER 14, 1979

Dear dear Lisa,

You are such a beautiful person to have shared your most private feelings with me in the hopes that you could in some way help me.

You are very dear to me Lisa and I feel that you do know it, but it is still too soon in our relationship for you to fully know the scope of all you mean to me.

I cried and cried over all the love that spilled from your words on those sheets of paper and shall reread them many times over. I have already read your letter about fifteen times.

I know all your feelings because I have felt them all *from a very young age until today.* I also think I know the answers now. However, knowing and *doing something about it* are two entirely different areas. You don't have to let food get you down. You can control your life. The problem can be conquered, corrected, and permanently erased in your case because you are so young, and "NOW IS THE TIME."

I only hope that when Vicki and I move to California (I can't believe you were only two years old the last time I saw you) we can have long talks, and I can give you the benefit of my experiences and help you so that you will *at long last* learn to like Lisa and appreciate her for the beautiful human being she is.

Eating is only a symptom. The cause is much deeper.

It is hard to believe that I started this letter the day I called you on the phone, but I have had a great many things to take care of. I have thought about you daily, but have not been able to get back to you.

I must admit I am a little discouraged. I have reached a plateau after losing twelve pounds and still feel huge. I try to walk at lunch time, but it is not always easy to get out. One of the girls is out of the office, etc., that kind of thing. At night it is dark. I will have to try and find a way. I am doing above the waist exercises daily and they seem to be helping somewhat.

All I can say is keep up the good attitude, exercise, and much love to you. I am so grateful you found out that I was in O.A. in New York and knew that your own California Overeater's Anonymous experience would make us soulmates. I would make this longer, but I finally want to get it into the mail.

> Much love always honey,
> *Aunt Judith*

DECEMBER 16, 1979

I guess I have to let things happen to actually believe that they are possible. I suppose that's why I gained back the weight that I lost last summer. I had to show myself that I could put it back on.

I guess that's why I had to take that one bite. I didn't believe that I wouldn't be able to stop. After that first jelly bean, man, that was it. So, I guess, you learn by trial and error. Well, now that I truly believe that I do have a disease maybe I can begin to cure it.

As they say in O.A., *without exception,* abstinence is the most important thing in my life!

West Valley High School
Abuela School District

OFFICE OF PRINCIPAL
THE PARENT FACULTY CLUB
MUSIC BOOSTERS

Dec. 17, 1979

TO WHOM IT MAY CONCERN:

I would like to take this opportunity to recommend Lisa Messinger, currently a senior at our high school, as a student of the highest caliber and potentially a great addition to the studentbody of U.S.C.

As Lisa's counselor I have watched her progress over four years and it would be difficult for me to imagine any student having as fine a high school career as Lisa has had. In terms of academic accomplishment, Lisa has maintained a straight A (4.0) average in a difficult and demanding program. Additionally, she has exemplified herself in the area of speech and has won the outstanding student award at out school.

Having taught Lisa in the classroom, I can speak with authority when I say that Lisa exemplifies the best qualities of scholarship and academic enthusiasm.

However, Lisa's academic abilities are only a part of what makes her such a fine candidate. Even more important are Lisa's personal qualities. She displays a concern for others and maturity uncommon in people her age, and is able to inter-act successfully with all types of people. Additionally, Lisa has a fine sense of humor and is able to keep life in perspective.

Recently, Lisa has decided on a tentative career choice in the field of broadcasting. Her exceptional verbal abilities and ease with people lead me to believe that this is an appropriate choice for her. Hopefully, you will be able to see the excellence we see in Lisa and will accept her into your program.

Thank you,

Robert Fraisse
Counselor

DECEMBER 20, 1979

The first page of one of my many blank writing journals.

This collection of thoughts is hereby dedicated to:
The new me.
The product of all my hopes and dreams.
The contented person that I, in due time, *will* become.

The first entry in the new journal.

I am going to give myself a present. I can't say it is for my eighteenth bithday, although, of course, it is. I can't say it's for Christmas or Hanukkah, but it is. I can't say it's given in the spirit of the new year, 1980, but a sense of beginnings is a part of it. I can't say it's a graduation present, although I am graduating on more than one level.

My present is, in a sense, in celebration of all these occasions. But to work it's got to be much more than that. I am giving myself my life. Control of it. Pride in it. The joy of living it day to day. I was going to say that I'm giving myself back my life. But then I realized that I'm not at all sure that I ever really had it.

I want it. Losing weight is only a tool that I will use to find the happiness and confidence that is in store for me. Before I will be able to see clearly, I will have to wipe away the clouds. When I am thin, I will be able to deal objectively and realistically with the true problems. I am unable to do that now.

I know that I can do it. I need to if I want to keep my sanity.

Happy New Year
Happy Birthday
Merry Christmas
Happy Hanukkah
Happy Graduation
HAPPY TOMORROWS
FULFILLED TODAY

JANUARY 4, 1980

I made an appointment for a tour guide interview at Universal Studios (que sera sera).
I get spurts of energy and then they fade. I'm going to pick up the

energy level of my lifestyle. Running? Maybe? It's neat out there before the sun, peaceful (but early)!

The high price of my impending college education is beginning to worry me.

JANUARY 4, 1980

It's one minute at a time. And this minute, 12:19P.M., I feel happy. So I guess for the moment I've got everything I want.

Something I read, and thought might be a morale booster, "Remember that the only thing that stands between you and success is you. Resolve to accept life as it comes and make the best of it, knowing that by doing so, you create an even better tomorrow."

JANUARY 6, 1980

Size seven. Size seven. Size seven. Here I am in Palm Springs and I am wearing size seven purple pants. Corduroy to be exact. And a beautiful mauve sweater. What are hours of dressing and make-up when it can turn out like this?

I have been kissed by a football player. A college football player. A rugged, curly haired, adorable football player. With a gorgeous physique.

Pecked, yes. Really kissed, no. Why did I turn my cheek? I dance with him all night, even after my parents leave the hotel disco, and then I turn my cheek. What is wrong with me? I was all ready for a tongue. I saw him coming at me outside my hotel room. I saw the mouth open. I saw the tongue. I thought, "This guy's 19. This time I'm gonna do it. No touchy, no feely, just the tongue." And I didn't.

But I don't really care, because I'm getting out of my purple pants and I'm going to sleep and I'm really not the least bit unhappy!

JANUARY 10, 1980

Here I stand at the crossroads of my life. I am at an ending and a beginning. I am at a vital point.

I look back. I see years of disgust, anguish, insecurity, tears, unfulfillment.

I know that I am about to embark on an exciting, lifelong journey. I am packing my mental bags and am on the brink of moving on. As I look ahead I see the first rays of sunshine and in the distance a rainbow.

I know that once I take that first step there is no turning back, my life will begin.

I am scared, but here I go. One quick glance back, and a sigh of relief. Life, here I come.

JANUARY 12, 1980

Lisa's New Life!

MEAL PLAN

Breakfast:
 1 fruit
 1 bread
 1 meat
 1 fat

Snack:
 1 fruit

Lunch:
 vegetables (unlimited)
 1 fruit
 1 bread
 2 meats
 1 fat

Dinner:
 vegetables (unlimited)
 1 fruit
 1 bread
 3 meats
 1 fat

NO SWITCHING AROUND OF FOODS. ALWAYS EAT AT SAME PLACE WHEN AT HOME. KEEP A FOOD DIARY.

EXERCISE PROGRAM

Jogging:
 Every morning. Start at two times around block. Progress as ready.

Home Work Out:
 Once each day, after school.

Health Club Exercise Class:
 Every day! Preferably the 6:30P.M. class.

Shopping Mall Ice Skating:
 One hour each weekday. Preferably from 12:00—1:00P.M.

Tennis:
Once on Sundays. During the week, as much as possible.

Bike Riding:
Once on Sundays for at least one hour and five miles.

JANUARY 16, 1980

I smiled before I went to sleep tonight. I know tomorrow is going to be a bright and beautiful day, a new chance that will bring me closer to my new life.

JANUARY 24, 1980

What in the hell is the matter with me? This is supposed to be my new life. It's already working, somewhat. I look pretty good. I feel pretty good.

However, a one pound of peanut M&M's, Miss Messinger, is not in your new life plan. No. No. No. Why the hell did you eat them? Sure, they were for your birthday party tonight. Right. Your parents have already bought enough food for thirty more people than the thirty who have been invited. You were supposed to be taking your SAT's, not be on a sugar high.

Granted, a 4.0 GPA may not force you to perform magnificently on SAT's, but a sugar rush and shaking hand do not make great test takers.

What the hell is the matter with you? You are doing okay, and bam, you're flat on your back. Shape up.

JANUARY 30, 1980

"Would you care to join me in the bathroom?" Not your run of the mill question. However, I assure you it was prompted more out of desperation than a desire for companionship. The party was ending. My eighteenth birthday party gala was almost "kaput," as was any chance for my romantic future. You see, Perry Schwartz was about to walk out the door taking all of my starry-eyed dreams with him.

I had to do something. It was now or never. I opted for the now. That's when I dragged him into the bathroom, our only place of refuge. In his eyes, was that the desire I had so often dreamed of or was it just fear? We've all heard tales of love-starved women attacking innocent young men in deserted powder rooms.

At any rate, I popped the question. And after a slight deliberation, he popped the answer, he would be "honored" to escort me to the school's Sadie Hawkins' dance. Dreams come true. Wishes are granted. Prayers are answered. The boy of my dreams, quite literally, was interested, semi-interested, or, at least, showed a flicker of interest.

I had plotted, planned, mapped out, lived out that moment a thousand times in my imagination. In fact, it was that play acting that gave me courage and confidence. Well, what I lacked in courage and confidence, I made up for in adrenalin.

Now, I'm a firm believer in the power of illusion. I'm also a firm believer in the power of pine-scented Lysol. I'm really not quite sure which did the trick.

JANUARY 30, 1980

Dear Lisa,

Just a word of thanks for inviting me to your birthday party. I really enjoyed myself as I am sure everyone else did as well. I am really glad I went and am looking forward to seeing you again soon.

Love,
Perry

FEBRUARY 24, 1980

Wow! That's about the only adjective that truly describes my feelings. Or maybe devastated. I think I'm in shock or a tailspin or something. I have certainly never felt this way before. It's a layman's guess, but I think I may be in love. I don't believe it. That's the first time I've admitted it even to myself. How come after all of this time knowing each other things seem to be happening so fast? I feel so inexperienced. The fact that Perry probably is too doesn't console me. He seems to catch on fast.

God! He likes me. After all of this time, it doesn't seem real! I have never been so nervous and reacted in such a way. The pains in my stomach have been unreal. They almost work as a sexual alarm system.

Sex? Hmmmm. It crossed my mind last night that he could be *the* first. But I trust him and his judgment so much.

Because I want it to work so much, I get too tense. Before the Sadie Hawkins' dance tonight nothing. Now, he's kissed me about eight times (count 'em, eight!). I kissed him once. And, brother, if holding my hand can make me go limp, I don't know what the big stuff is going to do. His arms around me slow dancing close . . . I like it all. I'm afraid, scared. He's so sweet and *handsome.* Everything I see I like.

I wonder how he's feeling. Talking abstractly a few weeks ago, as friends only, we both said we didn't want to get involved with anyone right now. But now it's on such a personal level.

What next? I am so confused! (But it's a nice kind of confusion.)

MARCH 20, 1980

I am very happy! All of those times I thought I was on the verge of something, and nothing! Then all of a sudden happiness crept up on me!

I've never looked or felt better. I think I am in love with Perry. If it isn't, it's the closest I've ever come.

I've grown up . . . in more ways than one!

I really am happy!

MARCH 21, 1980

Well. Well. Well. You know that experience I wanted behind me, it's behind me. I must say I think my sexual attitude is very healthy.

Although the Big Event hasn't been staged yet, I feel as though I know more about it.

It was right. It was natural. I would say I love Perry but I am not sure what love is.

What I do know is that I feel more deeply, and care more about him, and really truly like him more than anyone I've ever met.

So, whatever happens I will not regret last night. It was part of my growing up cycle. It is a part of my adult life.

MARCH 24, 1980

Have I been taking things for granted? Maybe I shouldn't trust my judgment so much. This is all so new to me. I don't want to make a wrong move. Perry has never told me how he feels. I mean in three words or less: i.e., "I love you." "I like you." "Bug off." Of course, he has said he likes me. No shit! (I'm getting vulgar in my old age.) Well, my mom said that my dad wouldn't say it for a long time either, and look at them, they've been married almost 30 years. I don't know if I am in love or not, but I like the way I am feeling. Although, today I am a little anxious. I wonder if all his thinking will amount to, "Take a hike." No, he wouldn't hurt me. Intentionally, that is. At all costs the relationship is worth it. Now that I've finally got something special I'm not giving up so easily. Turn of thought: I surprise myself. My attitude about sex had always been liberal but abstract. Now the situation is personal. I can't believe how comfortable I was. It felt right. It is right.

I am so grateful that I don't have any hang-ups about this all-important part of life. (Hope he doesn't.)

Grateful, too, to my wonderful mom who makes it so easy. She must be one in a million. He is too. So am I.

You know, I was just thinking all of this is important, but what's really important is how I feel about myself. And even though I ate like a maniac today (insecurity), I like myself. I am worthwhile. I am a good person. I have a lot of added extra-special qualities. I'll make it. I forgive myself (for eating). If that isn't progress!

I love myself. God, I think I've just had an experience comparable to any "born again" experience. Better. Live!

Later

I eat to escape. Is it possible that I just realized this? Could I be that dense? Didn't I know it all the time? Shove in the food, turn on the TV and tune out; that's the pattern. Now that I'm eighteen, I can write my own excuse notes for school. Escape notes. Do the Winchell's donut run (1 dozen assorted), get the Haagen-Dazs (a pint of mint chocolate), a few cans of Coke and lie down in front of the soap operas in the guest room. Parents at work. Door closed. Just stay outside, Consuela. Don't clean in the guest room today or two days from now or next Tuesday. Lisa is occupying the guest room, Consuela.

MARCH 26, 1980

I just received my housing confirmation from USC. Soon my whole life will be dramatically changing (starting). I am looking forward to college life, but right now ain't so bad either. Whether I'm in love or not is not important. I am comfortable in a relationship (with a capital "R," as Perry so cutely put it). I am learning about life and about myself. I feel lucky to have someone so compatible and likable. Physically speaking, it is amazing how quickly I have adapted. I like it (which I never thought I would), but am not overcome with the heat of passion (which is what I thought would happen). Keeping control is no problem. I am comfortable. I think that somewhere out there is someone who will spark my passion, emotional and physical, and then I will know love. But for now I am content. For once, I am at the right place at the right time.

10:40 P.M.

Whew! I feel 100 percent better. Revived. Invigorated. Awake. Alive again. Boy, exercise really does make a difference. While I was in bed I was thinking, I can't wait until tomorrow to get back on track after blowing it today by overeating. Then I thought, I could still get something done tonight. I'm glad I did. Wow, I didn't go Saturday, Sunday, Monday, Tuesday or Wednesday, didn't lift a muscle. I felt awful, tired, cranky. Now I feel better. I shouldn't bite the hand . . . This health club really shaped me up. I shouldn't slack off, or it'll be Flabsville! I think I'll boogie a bit before bed. Exercise is where it's at.

11:06 P.M.

Well, I just "discoed down" and I feel great. This is the *best* therapy. It really is an attitude reverser. Before, I felt lazy and fat like I wouldn't be able to get back into it. Well, I did great. I want to do my workout again before bed.

Tomorrow, here I come!

MARCH 27, 1980

MY FOOD PLAN

Breakfast:		Lunch:		Dinner:	
1 bread	70	1 bread	70	1 bread	70
1 meat	90	2 meats	130	2 meats	130
1 fruit	60	1 fat	40	1 fat	40
	220	vegies	free	vegies	free
			240		240

TOTAL: 700 calories

MARCH 30, 1980

Well, well, well. If I didn't know better, I'd say Perry is most definitely in love with me. But, of course, I know better. I'm not ruling out the possibility, though. (He did say he didn't know.) What the hell? Why label it? The feelings are great! He cares. I care. We're both lucky, two prudes in a pod *quickly* adapting!

I forgive myself. I've got a lot going for me. Why blow it by eating?

MARCH 31, 1980

1:31 A.M.

Alone in house. Perry just left. Feel fine. A real make out artist. I like it. No passion. Well, maybe a little bit.

APRIL 5, 1980

I am finally alone. There is, finally, something so personal I will not tell. It is my decision. My choice. Not Perry's. Not Mom's. Mine. Right now, I feel that I will abstain. Of course, I reserve the right to change my mind. First, because he's not said he loves me. He's not sure he does. But he does. If he were madly in love with me, I would. But he's not that type. I love him, but I'm not madly in love either.

What we have is very special. It doesn't come along every day. Some people never find it. We are lucky. However, I will not risk pregnancy, and even with every precaution there is still that possibility. Right now it's just not worth it to either of us.

How do I feel? I feel capable, normal, a little aggressive. I guess I'll just have to take life one day at a time.

Good idea.

APRIL 7, 1980

I feel so lucky. I have such a wonderful boyfriend, such an open relationship. We feel the same way about so many important things. Sex. That's important. We are having a physical relationship. I've been wanting to say that. I feel so comfortable. However, not comfortable

40

enough to go "all the way," although I can see how some girls could. He's got *some* build!

I am in love, in a way, but I don't know if I'm in love with Perry or with the idea of being in love. I have a feeling it's the latter. Oh well, I feel great. I never could understand what "making out" was. Needless to say I do now, and I like it. I really do. Shock!

If Rod Burke asked me out, would I go? Probably, since Perry made a point of saying no commitments.

I don't ever want to forget how I feel now. *Content!* A feeling relatively new to me.

APRIL 7, 1980

1:04 A.M.

I can't sleep. Maybe I drank too much diet soda today. I was hungry and had a craving for cereal (even my cravings are nutritious now), so I had a bowl. It's nice to be able to eat without blowing it. It's a good feeling to have some leeway. I must admit I've been feeling pretty wonderful lately, but it's a different kind of wonderful. I've been up and down, but the ups have been prevailing.

The prom is in fifty days. How nice to have someone so special at such a special time. He will ask me. (He'd better.) I know it will be a beautiful night, even better than the Sadie Hawkins' dance, if that's possible. Grad night, too, will be a ball, a far cry from last year's with that jerk. I'll ask Perry to that, if time starts running out.

Perry is so handsome. Gorgeous, dark curly hair (which my fingers always end up running through). Beautiful (an understatement) green eyes. Dark, smooth complexion that's always tan. (No pimples!) Broad, broad shoulders. Arms with just the right kind of muscles. Cute, cute hairless chest (the best kind). Flat, hard stomach. Oops, I forgot those big, nicely curved lips and long, luscious tongue. And, of course, those huge, masculine hands. Sexy, sexy, tan, hairy, long, muscular legs. In other words, no complaints!

Understandably, the newness of romance has taken up much of my thoughts. I catch myself thinking about him a lot. Thinking is one thing, but I don't want to bore people. Boredom hasn't been a problem for me lately. I've been excited both mentally (he is the most intelligent person I know) and physically. Physically, I have been discovering quite a lot about myself. I am by no means inhibited. I am in control, but not inhibited, and very spontaneous—traits I thought I lacked, especially in this area. I like kissing a lot and everything else (almost) too. I think I will like "it" too, but *we* have decided not to get "totally" involved. I am satisfied with this decision.

Honestly, I am feeling more satisfied with most things lately. I'm finally living in the present, not contemplating the future and daydreaming about what college will be like. Believe it or not, I am happy with myself. I like the way I look. I really think 122 pounds is okay. This is not to say that I'm still not trying to improve. I am. The difference is that I'm not obsessed with losing weight, merely determined. I realize that what I've got is pretty good and I can only get better. I have not forgotten, though, that it is all too easy to slip and binge again, especially when over-confidence and the feeling that things have always been dandy sets in. This is not true. I've made myself miserable in the past. I'm walking a fine line, and it would be easier to fall than continue on the tightrope. This must always be in the back of my mind, that refraining from binging is a daily accomplishment.

I won't take it for granted.

What I went through to get Perry taught me that when you really want something you have to go for it. Then, once you get it, it takes hard work to keep the sailing smooth. But, it is *definitely* worth it!

APRIL 8, 1980

Wow! I'm really shaping up! All this going to the club after school and exercising on my own is finally paying off. My upper arm is smaller, so are legs. Stomach is pretty hard, face a bit thinner. Don't know what I weigh at the moment, probably about 121. That's okay, though I still want to lose.

God, do I have a handsome boyfriend! I have good taste. Today when Perry came over, whoa! He looked very sexy to me. Cha, cha, cha.

We've been kissing on the run lately, but it's fun, and the pecks have turned into flicks. I like.

I can't wait until the prom. *Boy*, am I happy.

APRIL 9, 1980

Forget the past.
Nothing is irreversible, not even eating 10,000 calories.

Life is an exciting adventure
that starts anew each day.

You've got it, so do something with it!

APRIL 11, 1980

I do not understand myself to say the least! So cocky, mentally that is. I fell from my tightrope.

Right now, I'm getting up and brushing myself (my ego) off. Or at least I think so. Who can say for sure? I know that I hate living in the pits, and I don't ever have to be there. I have control over it.

The bottom line is that I feel great when I abstain. Yes, abstain! That Overeater's Anonymous word. Ominous, but true. It's not being perfect or inflexible. It is abstaining from compulsive overeating. It's not worth it to let go and get flabby. I care too much about myself.

APRIL 15, 1980

I am happy. I could be miserable, but I'm not. I have such good friends. Perry is such a wonderful boyfriend! They all stuck up for me. Because of their support I didn't overeat to solve this problem with the speech team. A few people, according to my friends, can't stand me because I win and win and win on my own without selling my soul to the ''group.''

In terms of eating, past performance was forgotten. I didn't think about all of the times I did gorge to escape from these kind of confrontations. I feel good about today. A potentially rotten experience turned out okay!

APRIL 18, 1980

I feel good! Perry, a wonderful boy, likes me. I feel like I'm in love, but who knows? I've felt like saying it, but I know I won't unless he does. He's so cute. We're so comfortable. We go together.

I like. I like. I like.

APRIL 19, 1980

Saturday 3:00 A.M.

I am definitely in love! I feel fantastic! This has been the best night of my life. Perry told me all he saw in me: pretty, brains, ambition, and asked me to the prom.

He feels for me! He loves me, I can tell. We won't say it yet, but someday. He's the most wonderful boy I ever met, and I love him.

Tonight was beautiful.

APRIL 25, 1980

I'm a very happy girl. It just dawned on me, I'm starting a weight loss program without being miserable and without being dumpy and bulgy. I'm happy and I look fine. What a switch, but it's that switch that will bring success. I know my goal, 110 pounds, and I will seek it realistically. I like what I'm starting out with, so I can only get better! What an attitude.

God, am I ever in love. I love love. This is terrific. Even when I'm down, I'm up. Perry's so right! Not perfect by any means, but that's what makes it so good and real, I know I haven't gone mushy. Well, I had my first bed experience. (Water yet!) It was a lot more comfortable than the couch, and especially the car. The prom is something to look forward to, but I like every day. They seemed numbered, like we're coming to the end of one life (high school) and the beginning of another (college). Could it be that we'll be the one overlapping link in each other's two lives?

What a beautiful thought.

APRIL 25, 1980

I am beginning a weight loss program. Seriously. My goal weight is 110 pounds. The program is 1000 calories a day: three meals, one snack, or less.

Signed,
Lisa Messinger
(No frills this time.)

MAY 1, 1980

Weight: 122 pounds

Breakfast:
1 tbsp. peanut butter	90
2 slices thin bread	70
½ c. grapefruit juice	40
	200

Lunch:
tuna fish	90
diet mayo	40
1 bun	130
strawberries	30
	290

Snack:
yogurt	200

Dinner:
1 egg	90
1 regular bread	65
	155

Total: 845 calories

MAY 1, 1980

Bust: 36½''   Upper leg: 21½''

Waist: 26½''   Lower leg: 12½''

Hips: 36½''   Calf: 8''

Midriff: 34''   Lower arm: 8¼''

Upper arm: 10¼''   36½''—26½''—36½''

MAY 3, 1980

Saturday 5:41 A.M.

I think I'm confused. I don't know what the hell to think or do. One thing seems right, going out with only Perry. I also want to play the field, but I don't really want that. I was testing Perry. He said we should see other people as well as each other, and I said let's just keep seeing each other. He didn't back down and neither did I. Compromise. What happened to compromise? I guess you just can't compromise on some things. Why does he have to be so analytical and intelligent and logical?

God, *he thinks he's in love with me.* This is too much. And I said that I think I love him too. He *can't* stop going out with me, even if he thinks we should see other people too. *Love, love, love.* God, I want to be in love.

My first real orgasm. And I passed the bathing suit barrier. I actually wore one and got a compliment! I asked for it! Okay, okay, okay. Just take your time and think about it. This is GREAT!

MAY 5, 1980

Realizations: there are no more fat pockets on my legs (''beautiful'' legs according to Perry, my beau). No more perpetual pimples. The ones that were always there . . . gone! Firm arms! No wishing, it just happened. No, I guess I did it.

Love . . . I'm in it.

What do I do? Take one day at a time. Remain calm. As they said, you're a calm person. Keep your calm! HE LOVES ME!

MAY 27, 1980

Bust: 36½''	Upper arm: 10¼''
Waist: 26''	Upper leg: 21½''
Hips: 36''	Lower leg: 12½''
Midriff: 33''	Calf: 8''
	Lower Arm: 8¼''

MAY 30, 1980—PROM DAY

WOW!

ME AND PERRY!!!
He couldn't keep his hands off me.
Hollywood Denny's hand-holding
Beach walking kisses
Beach blanket caresses
Jeremy's breakfast bash
Car in front of house under street light, me under him.

46

JUNE 6, 1980

Dreams can become realities.
Believe. Believe. Believe.
Not binging is not easy, but it's worth it!
You've come a long way, Baby!

JUNE 12, 1980

I've never felt better.

I didn't truly know Perry. He's so sincere. We compromised. We decided we could date other people as well as each other. After we made up, we went to the beach with Jeremy, Laura and Glen. (Me at the beach in a teeny weeny red bikini, that's what I call progress!)

JUNE 13, 1980—GRADUATION

Well, I was great! Not nervous giving the graduation speech at all. To me this was a beautiful night. Everything was right, being with the Schwartz's and such a good friend like Leslie.

Grad night at Disneyland—well, I'll never look at "Small World" and "Haunted Mansion" in quite the same way. Perry couldn't seem to keep his hands off me on those rides or any other time, and I loved every minute of it. I couldn't keep my eyes off him. He looked so NICE. Such a NICE BOY.

Our little Swedish pancake breakfast party at my house was fun, but it's the "dessert" that I'll always remember.

What next? Will Perry and I end up together or apart? I'll just play it by ear.

Voted "Most Likely to Succeed." Boy, did I feel great (and surprised)!

JUNE 13, 1980

Dearest Lisa,

Hi! If you fall asleep over this I hope you find it and read it. I just want to tell you again how absolutely magnificent you were. You are beautiful (as always) and smart, witty, mature and as I've thought always too, "most likely to succeed." Well, what more could you ask for? Valedictorian, speeches, beautiful friends, you're a very lucky and successful girl. Now here's something I've never told anyone except you now, you are everything I utmost desire to be and achieve when I get older. Looks, brains, emotions, personality, all around exceptional. You're a treasure to everyone you meet. Lately, I've felt close to you and I hope this summer holds more of that closeness in store for us. I wouldn't want to be in California (although I often have second thoughts about mom and I having moved here) without someone like "specifically you," Lisa. I just wanted you to know how I felt. Although we vary in age, I still feel we have such good times together, and although your upcoming steps on life's winding roads will be tough ones, unique ones, remember I'll always be here and I'll always think of you *very often*. So take care because I love you so very much.

Love,
Vicki

JUNE 16, 1980

Sick and in bed. I think I'll write a few pages to a hypothetical autobiography:

Rob Jeffries was the boy voted Most Likely to Succeed in my senior class. He is your standard jockish, scholarly Aryan: baseball, football and soccer varsity, and a 3.8 grade point average. He is rich, nice, and fairly straight. Voted Most Popular Boy and Prom King.

The girl voted Most Likely to Succeed should have been Kari Tamner. She was Associated Student Body President, nice, smart, blonde and blue eyed. A four year cheerleader, the only thing she had in common with the other cheerleaders was a great pair of legs. She is going to study communications at U.C., San Diego.

When I arrived at school on Friday, June 13th, graduation morning, I was shocked to find out that Kari Tamner had not won and that I had. I was flocked by people I had barely spoken to in my four years of high school asking me why I had not been at the award's breakfast I had swept.

"God, you won Succeed, Best Public Speaker, and Best Student. Everyone was wondering where you were."

"Everyone" wondering where *I* was? I had been home in bed thinking how no one in the world, let alone the senior class, should give a damn about a worthless person like me.

I had gotten out of bed that morning, unlike so many mornings before, only because Dean Belgetti had said that if we didn't come to the final graduation rehearsal we wouldn't graduate. I, of course, lived by everything Dean Belgetti said, and besides, I was the graduation speaker.

On the mornings I didn't go to school, I'd stay home and watch soap operas, cry, and eat Winchell's donuts by the dozen, Haagen-Dazs ice cream by the pint, and Swanson TV dinners by the tray. It seemed like I spent half of my senior year in this manner. The other half I spent writing my own excuse notes (allowed once you were eighteen), and dropping courses right and left in order to preserve my status as a 4.0 student, not to mention my slot as a 1980 valedictorian.

I was compulsive about those sorts of things, a perfectionist by birth. My mother tells me I cleaned my own diapers and burped myself. She may exaggerate, but I've taken over the exaggerating here. I've made my life one great big exaggeration.

Friday, June 13th, by the way, was one of the best days of my life. Not because I graduated from high school and spent the night prancing around Disneyland with my boyfriend, but because I was succumbing to the tonsillitis and pink eye that would keep me drugged and dozing for the next several days. You see, when you're drugged and dozing you can't do much of anything, let alone eat. For the last several days I have subsisted on lemonade and popsicles.

Since my diet has consisted of more sugar than a sugar commercial, I thought I was gaining weight. You can imagine my surprise, therefore, when I stepped on the scale and saw in front of me the number 117, a virtual miracle. For most of my pubescent life I have hovered somewhere between 122 and 128 pounds. That is why Friday, June 13th was one of the best days of my life.

(To be continued, someday.)

3. Itsy-Bitsy Teeny-Weeny Polka-Dot Bikini

JUNE 20, 1980

You are strong.
You will make it.
You can roll with the punches.
You *are* a winner.

I feel so proud. I don't really know why. These things just seem to happen. Even though I have tonsillitis, I know that I've worked hard for this. I tried on my leotards, without tights, and could see no stomach. Wow! Bikini looks nice also. Too much! So much of it is psychological, how you mentally see yourself. I'm walking on a slippery floor and, boy, would it be easy to slip. But I know where I'm going.
Wow.
Weight: 117 pounds

JUNE 24, 1980

A milestone. Today, I became an employee, a page, at a television station! Another phase of my life has begun. I knew I could do it, but doing is different from knowing. There is no stopping me now. I think I will make it as far as I want to go. Timing is everything. Wow!

Another thing worth recording: I received a $4000 honor scholarship.

JUNE 27, 1980

Something is happening to me. It is wonderful, it is dynamic, and, at the same time, it is confusing and scary. I feel different. I think I am emerging as a person, an individual. I don't know exactly what I was before. It's as though I had no personality. I was dull. I was blah. I thought I was grown-up and mature before, but now I feel as though I am really growing.

Although I feel that in essence this has been a day by day very gradual process that I initiated in October, I think three major experiences (events) were catalysts: getting the job, losing weight, and my relationship with Perry. All of these are basically wonderful and, to a large extent, a result of my own personal push. Yet each area creates questions and uncertainty.

When I heard I had gotten the job I cried. I had done something that deep down I always believed I could. All of a sudden, it seemed my life had been changed (by me). I walked off the street into that studio, a studio where they said almost 3,000 people a year applied for those page jobs. The future went from being an attainable dream to an attainable reality.

My confidence in myself has made this possible. Where has this confidence come from? It seems relatively new, and yet, I know it's been long in coming. I'll tell you the greatest joy, I like myself, not just one facet, but the whole package. In fact, I love myself, and I feel this is unchangeable. I may go up and down, but I have my own respect now. I think I am beautiful. And although I've written that, I don't feel conceited. This is the way it is. I am a beautiful, pretty, intelligent, talented, motivated, sweet person. I like my body. Although this is not the most important fact, as of today I weigh 115½ pounds. I've worked for it. My long time weight goal is in sight. I want to protect it once I reach it, so I've decided to go back to the nutritionist I went to two years ago. There I can get a balanced, nutritious maintenance plan.

I love the way I look. I feel I really deserve this. It was not handed to me on a silver platter. Although some say I was always pretty, I don't think I was. (Maybe I was just blinded by self-hatred.) I feel I've molded myself.

I know that looks aren't everything. I thought they were. The personality I never thought I had is emerging. I'm not sure yet what it is. I can be funny and witty. I can be spontaneous. I can be cute. I can be sexy. I can be honest. I can enjoy sex. I can enjoy life. And I can enjoy myself.

I am confused about my relationship with Perry. How do you know if someone is right for you? Through this relationship I have learned to open up and be myself more, yet sometimes I feel like I'm not being myself. He's a very lucky boy to have me.

What makes me such a motivated, goal-oriented person? At eighteen I feel miles ahead of my peers and friends in this area. I can't sit still. I can't be a camp counselor or a waitress when the world is out there and I am ready to conquer it. What sets me apart? At any rate, I know the things I am doing are making me happy.

All along I've tried to do the "best" thing, the "right" thing, tried to be the best. Now I just want to be me, no matter what it takes, no matter what I have to do, what images I have to shatter, what approval I must forsake.

I am on the brink of self-discovery and I feel as though a great load has been lifted from my shoulders. I am free to breathe.

JUNE 28, 1980

5:19 A.M.

I have accomplished so much regarding my weight and self-image. Looking back, it's taken about a year. Before that everything was overshadowed by self-hatred and insecurity. My first hostess job last summer made me feel somewhat attractive, yet toward the end I was sneaking rolls, soup, cheesecake and chocolate syrup (yuk.) At my second hostess job I also ate bakery items and rolls and bread, and that was as recently as last February.

JUNE 29, 1980

This job is going to be *great*. Can you believe it? I got a size five uniform. I was wearing my size three purple pants the day I got the job, the day I said to the head of the page staff, "If I don't get this job, I'll go to every studio in Hollywood and knock on doors. And I'll get a job." I couldn't believe the things I said. It was like I caught fire the minute the guard said they were interviewing for pages. I knew if there were openings I could get a job. And I did. Last interview out of the whole group and first hired. Wheee!

This job is going to be *great*. A cameraman already told me I was beautiful, looked like a beautiful Spanish señorita, and asked me to go sailing (which I won't).

But it is a lot more than this attention. Where was I today? On the set of a national talk show having Patrick Duffy of "Dallas" tell me, "just keep smiling and you'll make it," as he walked out onto national television.

I am here. I made it in. I am surrounded by "the beautiful people," and by some miracle I have become one of them.

JULY 2, 1980

Things seem to be going very well now. Nevertheless, the past casts a shadow I can't ignore. I have a disease. I am a compulsive overeater.

Although the symptoms, outer flab and inner insecurity, may have disappeared, the germ of the disease remains. Just as a diabetic must take his daily doses of insulin, I must take my daily doses of positive thinking.

I am me and that is good enough. It never was before. Who am I? That is a question that I am answering and will continue to answer every day for the rest of my life. Sometimes my findings will be pleasing, sometimes not. But I will be accepting. I accept myself.

I have confidence and strength. I am only beginning to tap these resources. By losing weight I have conquered my own inner demon. Consequently I will never be defeated by life.

I can't say that I am used to myself yet. I can't say that I truly know myself yet. But day by day I come face to face with a welcome stranger and a new found friend.

JULY 4, 1980

An analogy came to mind today. My room reflects me, not only the possessions, but the manner in which it is kept. To the eyes of others it is always perfect. If it is not up to par, no one sees it. Period. Most of the time it is in a state of mess, clutter and confusion. I cannot seem to keep it up.

I used to project that same kind of "neat" image to the world. Every hair had its place, and every hair in its place. Smile, smile,

smile. Don't let anyone see you unless you look perfect. But what was underneath that false exterior? A mess. Anger, self-hatred, self-punishment and denial. Clutter.

Luckily, or purposely, I am changing. Letting my hair down, or more appropriately, in my case, putting it up. Letting loose and letting go. It's hard not being so hard on myself.

I am less than perfect. It's also hard to admit, but now I'm not sure what I'm striving for. Before, it was perfection pure and simple (or, I should say, polluted and difficult—impossible). What I want now is to be the best me I can be. How do I know when I get there?

JULY 6, 1980

The ultimate test: Can I really go to a roller disco wearing a rainbow tube top?

(Scratch that! We couldn't go.)

I look in the mirror and I like what I see. In the past this would have seemed like a miracle. Now at times I'm even blasé. I realize, however, that I could never really be blasé about it. I worked too hard. This *is* a tremendous (or rather ''trim''-endous) accomplishment.

I look inward, and I like what I am beginning to sense, an assertiveness. Passiveness is passé. Shyness is turning to sensitivity. As my shell grows tougher—I can take almost anything now—I grow softer. My growth actually has been phenomenal. I realize now that I have never really known myself. It was as if I had hated a stranger, someone I had never taken the time or courage to get to know.

Well, now it is a totally different ball game. I am continually hitting singles, doubles, triples and even home runs. I won't forget my past strike record, however. While I appreciate the cheers from the crowd they are not essential. My own congratulations mean more than all the applause in the world.

This, I think, is a phase. I am discovering my identity. When I grow to know myself more fully I will be comfortable and content.

I am special. I may be good. I may be bad. But I am special. Deep inside I know that I will make it in every way.

JULY 7, 1980

My life is consistently wonderful. This is not to say that everything is coming up roses. I am the rose. It may be raining upon me. The ground around me may turn to mud. I may be left to grow alone, yet, I, myself, remain calm, peaceful, strong, stable and subtly beautiful.

I am full of pride. I have done a great thing by losing weight and continuing to do so. I am only beginning. Life holds beautiful things in store for me because that's what *I* hold in store for life!

JULY 8, 1980

Bust: 36''		Thigh: 20''!	
Waist: 25''!		Lower leg: 12½''	
Hips: 35''		Calf: 7½''	
Abdomen: 32''!		Upper arm: 10''!	

JULY 8, 1980

I have come full circle. Mine is a life worth living. I have achieved. I have accomplished. I have become. I have arrived.

Life is no longer torment. Life is no longer misery. Life is no longer punishment. Life is no longer repression, denial, self-hatred or insecurity.

Life is mine. Life is challenging. Life is adventure. Life is acceptance. Life is calm, serene and peaceful. Life is courage, strength and confidence. Life is joy beyond ecstasy. Life is love, simple in its complex intricacies. Life is living. I have grown-up. I have taken the reins of my life in my own hands. I grabbed control.

Day by day, moment by moment, setback by setback, goal by goal, pound by pound, I created the love I now feel for myself. Without being able to foresee the future I believed in myself. I was not my ideal person or weight, yet I sensed my potential and never gave up on the toughest enigma, myself.

So much of the growth was subconscious. It took place, oh so gradually, beneath the surface. Before, I had only tried to alter, repair and cleanse that surface, never even guessing at the special fountain that lay deep within.

I am only beginning to tap that fountain.

JULY 15, 1980

There is nothing wrong with the way I am eating or not eating.
Everyone keeps saying I should eat more. I tell them I am not hungry.

I am finally 113 pounds. I am finally a size three. I bring my can of
chocolate liquid protein to work everyday, and when I reapply my
make-up on my break I drink it. I have two or three more cans a day.
I'll start eating again soon. Sometimes I eat a little, I've been not
eating for only about a month. I'm really not that hungry anymore.

I am thin. I am happy. And that's all that matters for now.

JULY 23, 1980

Well, well, well, life is always changing, isn't it? What I am about to
record is by no means a fact. It is just a reaction, an impression, that I
have as of today.

I think I may have put it in perspective (at least mentally). It was a
high school relationship. We are better friends now than ever. We
have a beautiful friendship. I think we were both so scared at the
newness before that we couldn't *really* get to know each other. We
were always concerned with such trivial, surface things. Now it's
easier to talk, really talk.

It is probably time to move on. Something has changed. The future.
Before I hoped Perry would be a big part of it. Now, I don't think he
will. Although I am by no means sure.

It was nice, and a growing experience.

But there's a whole world out there. It would be naive and foolish
to believe that there is only one person who can make you happy.

JULY 24, 1980

Things have truly fallen into place. I am whole, and I am beautiful.
Today, Greg Butler, a terrific person, became interested in me. What
will happen I am not sure. But he is extraordinary and extraordinarily
good (great) looking.

We have a date for tomorrow night.

My life is looking up.

JULY 25, 1980

Another momentous first date. Where it will lead who knows? What's more important is the here and now. Jumping from Perry to Greg is like jumping from one cutie-pie to another. I can't believe we've both been working as pages for over a month and had never even met before. What a kiss!

JULY 27, 1980

Surprise after pleasant surprise. I can't believe he called me so quickly, the minute I got home from San Diego even though it was so late. I think I am becoming involved (I am) with a very special (spectacular and unique) person. I am excited, and yet I am calm (and confident and competent). To say Greg is gorgeous is superficial. That's what his modeling and acting are for. However, there is so much more to him than that.

True, we've only known each other a short while, yet it is very comfortable. This is another measure—meter of my progress. I am different. I am fulfilling my potential. As he quite appropriately put it, "Sweet dreams."

JULY 28, 1980

2:14 A.M.

Well, Greg certainly is unique. I've never met anyone like him. Wow, I'm not sure what I think yet. I'll have to get to know him better.

I know, though, that when we have these marathon late night phone conversations, I am entranced. He does impressions. He talks to me like Jack Nicholson. But who needs anyone else? I am charmed. He is charming. At twenty, the oldest person I've been out with. He is so smooth; there's something very special there. He's on fire, like many of the pages, but more so. He is not just a pretty, vacant Bel-Aire boy. True, he's pretty. And he definitely comes from the "right side of the tracks." But he has the charisma and energy that would take him to the top of the business world regardless of where on the ladder he started.

This is a time in my life I will always remember. Everything should not be taken so seriously.

JULY 28, 1980

Bust: 35"!	Thigh: 19"!
Waist: 24"!	Lower leg: 11½"
Hips: 32"!	Calf: 8"
Abdomen: 29½"!	Upper arm: 10"

AUGUST 5, 1980

I am a different person. Both inside and out. I really haven't been aware of the full extent of my change.

I look different. I am a size three as opposed to a size seven or nine. Consequently my face and body are not the ones I was used to seeing (if I really did see).

As for my personality, it hasn't changed, it's emerged (because it wasn't there before). I *am* a different person.

I remember reading about how a former fatty must mourn for her "fat self," someone she has had such an intensive love-hate relationship with for so long. I also remember thinking that this did not apply to me. That was then; this is now. I believe I am grieving. It has begun to hit me that the old me is gone, really gone. I don't know where she is. She must be dead. A big part of me has died. Although, for the most part, I didn't like this person, I cared about her.

Not liking yourself is misery, but it becomes routine and almost comfortable. Now knowing yourself, however, is scary as hell. I'm terrified and yet confident that in time I will come to know the mysterious, compelling stranger that stares at me from the other side of the mirror.

AUGUST 7, 1980

3:00 A.M.

Putting things in their proper perspective is not an easy task. For example, I am not sure what I look like. Sometimes I see one thing (a fat, ugly person), sometimes another (a thin, pretty person). What is real? I am not sure. What do others see?

Everything is confusing. But I will keep hanging on, taking one day at a time and enjoying life.

I may be falling for Greg, a total cutie-pie. That, too, I will take as it comes.

AUGUST 9, 1980

Redirect that anger and reassess it. Greg didn't mean to upset you by not going with you to the party. Assess what's important, and then go for it. Don't waste time being mad or eating over being mad. Don't give up, no matter what.

Don't compromise and don't settle.

You can be the weight *you* want to be.

Do it. Your way.

AUGUST 10, 1980

Another crossroad along the path of self-discovery: I find that I can't just settle for being "thin" or "trim" or "fit" or "in good shape."

What is it, then, that I want, and is it realistic? Am I setting myself up for failure and self-defeat? I want to be a knock out! I want to be in great shape. I want to have a terrific figure. I want to look *fantastic* (and feel that way, too).

Truthfully, I am already pretty, slim and attractive. I have a very good figure. And my self-image has greatly improved. But, damn it, I am not going to stop short of my goal again. I will not sell myself short.

My goal is realistic because I am not aiming for perfection. Perfection has been a major flaw in my character. No more. I *am* human. I do make mistakes. But, I do think I can be better (not perfect, just better). What, in all honesty, I want is to be the very best I can be. Anything less is a cop-out.

I feel my potential is immense. Why stop at A− when you have A+ potential?

P.S. In order to squelch all fears of crazed dieting (i.e., anorexia) I will set a conscious weight that I will not go under (without serious consideration): 103 pounds.

AUGUST 12, 1980

Another journey begins.
Seek and you shall find: 103 pounds.

AUGUST 17, 1980

Boy, has my life changed. Me. Me has changed.

Perry. I love him. I do. I guess I jumped the gun when I thought our relationship was over. I don't know if I'm "in love" with him or if I just plain love him. We are so special, together and apart. We are and have been good for each other. After not seeing each other, when he kissed me and told me I looked beautiful, it felt right. (I knew I looked beautiful. After all, I was wearing a satin magenta size five jumpsuit!)

So it turned out for the best after all that Greg couldn't go to Janine's birthday party with me. I was mad, since she's my best friend and I wanted him to meet her. If he had come, though, I might never have re-discovered Perry. I decided that Perry is a beautiful boy who will someday be a beautiful man, who I may or may not have all of, but who I nevertheless will always remember.

AUGUST 18, 1980

First, I want to record Greg, my "other boyfriend" for posterity. Very nice. He's extremely good-looking. He's got "it," the "glow," which, incidentally, I've decided Perry has acquired, too, just as I have. Blonde (white blonde), straight, nicely cut hair. Big light blue eyes. Great smile. Charm. Nice nose. Six foot two inches. Very slim, but looks excellent in clothes and has excellent taste. He's a unique person who's beginning to grow on me. I like him. But I still have deep, special feelings for Perry. I don't know Greg well enough to make any judgments, but I'm glad he's around.

What am I doing? Foodmania has entered the picture again. Although there is a difference, I'm not guilt ridden. (Not that I'm thrilled.) I think I do it to deal with frustration, anger, fear of sexuality, anxiety over moving out and starting a new life in college. Okay, so you know partly why you do it, so *why* do it?

Lisa, you know what you have to do, you have to cut this shit out for good, you have to reach your ideal dream weight. You're so close.

60

And you, Lisa, can do anything. You are you, and that ain't chopped liver!

Why pull yourself down like today? Why couldn't you have just gone to Pierre's going away party? You swam. You sat by the pool in your skimpy bathing suit, and you knew you looked good. Yes, it was a lot different than parties of years before. Yes, you felt like a different person. Yes, it was weird. So Greg couldn't go, couldn't sit next to you at Pierre's beautiful Beverly Hills pool and spa. What's the big deal? These people are all wonderful and all your friends. Why did you have to stop at that Thrifty on the way. No, two candy bars might not have seemed like a big binge before, but now it's huge. And on the way home? A pint of Baskin-Robbins is right back down your old path. Things were supposed to be different now. At 112 pounds things are supposed to be different.

Something just hit me. I want to stop. For good. What is more important than anything in my life is to be an abstaining compulsive eater and to be able to eat, rather than just drinking liquid protein, and still be abstaining. (That seems to be losing its charm, judging by today.) This is the only thing that can separate the future from the past, tomorrow from today.

It is the most important thing in my life.

I will do it because I have to.

I love me.

AUGUST 21, 1980

I want to have no stomach.
I want a little butt.
I want skinny fingers.
I want a thin face.
I want firm boobs.
I want a *small* waist.
In other words—*I want it all.*
GO FOR IT!!!

Current Weight: 115 pounds.

AUGUST 26, 1980

What is happening? Am I losing sight of reality?

Stop fooling yourself.

Do you want to throw away your life? Stick a knife in your back? Give up freedom for slavery? It *is* your choice.

Is it finally hitting you? Food in excess is *poison.* It is.

A bag of chocolate chips. A whole bag of marshmallows. Come on! This is a problem that is not going to go away. Go ahead, cry. But you can *do* something.

You can be as strong as you can be, strong enough to forgive, not forget.

This condition is controllable. So learn how to control it.

In this case, the end (weight loss) does *not* justify the means (total starvation.) You thought it did.

Now you know a little better.

And you're learning every single minute.

AUGUST 31, 1980

I feel so gorgeous! Maybe I have only lost three pounds, but thin really is just as much a state of mind as of the body. It is, indeed, a state that must be fought for, protected and appreciated, whether consciously or unconsciously, every day of your life.

Taking off excess weight is no easy task. However, the true test, the real tough stuff, is keeping off the weight, and the negative self-image, permanently.

Feeling great takes work. Feeling lousy comes naturally; you don't have to work at it.

I'd rather work for the first option, and it *is* an option, a choice. Life is choices.

Positive thinking is *the* most valuable tool in a valuable life. A helpful motto for me has been:

> I will be what I will to be.
> I will do what I will to do.
> I want to be!
> I am.

I love life.

SEPTEMBER 1, 1980

Keeping it off is the hard part.
I didn't compulsively overeat.
Eating is not compulsively overeating.
I *am* beautiful.

SEPTEMBER 2, 1980

I am a product of myself.
I am not a product of chance.
I am not a product of nature.
I am my own artist, creator, designer.

4. College

SEPTEMBER 8, 1980

A new phase. Another one. College. Here I sit in my dorm room. Solid impressions have not yet set in. It is new and exciting. One interesting note: when asked to list our priorities others wrote, get good grades. For me there was no question, be happy.

Everything is an outgrowth of that state of mind. Other things fall into place. Well, I've changed. I do feel calm and peaceful.

Like, I can take it.

SEPTEMBER 15, 1980

Today I became a college student. But, oh, I have become so much more than that. I am finally thin. The calmness and serenity that come from that fact are a subtle backdrop to life now. The realization that ''I can'' has blended in. Happiness is only a part of it. Contentment is the key word. That is more inclusive. It's not like everything is wonderful all the time, but life, itself, is wonderful. It's true you may have to dig through tons of dirt to find a few diamonds, but that makes the digging worthwhile and gives it purpose, meaning and significance.

SEPTEMBER 24, 1980

I will be what I will to be.
I will do what I will to do.

I want to be.
I am.

SEPTEMBER 25, 1980

I hope my electric wok isn't stinking up the dorm room, but I can't
eat that dorm food. Meal ticket, meal ticket, go to waste. Tough luck.
I cried to my mom when I asked her to bring my wok and told her I
couldn't use my meal ticket except for cereal for breakfast. I felt so
bad that I was wasting their money—so much of it is being spent
here—but she said, "Don't worry about it. Just be happy." The point
is, though, if sometimes I'm going to eat normally and sometimes
drink my liquid protein (pretty expensive for me), then dinners have to
be light (chicken, vegetables, etc.). I'll cook them in my wok and wash
it out in the bathroom.

Mashed potatoes, bread, cake, cookies: forget it. I gained five pounds
in the first week and a half. There's no way that's going to happen to
me.

Not *me*. Not the girl who has suddenly become a potential campus
star. I mean I saw it coming this summer with the reaction I got at
my job, but this is incredible.

Nice looking guys asking me to dance. A lot of guys. Everywhere I
go I'm getting asked out. This is amazing. A dream.

And there's still Perry and Greg. And me, in my little blue alligator
sweater, a sweater girl finally, charming the pants off everybody.

Just hold on and enjoy the ride.

SEPTEMBER 27, 1980

". . . Despite the fact that I am meeting many new people every day,
I find that I miss you very much. I do hope to see you again soon, or
at the very least continue a correspondence if you do not wish to go
out anymore, but I hope you do."

Love,
Perry

SEPTEMBER 30, 1980

Love is confusing. I really don't understand the way I've been feeling. I was so depressed. I kept thinking about Perry, about us. I was hurt and upset that he didn't even call, let alone see me, before I moved into the dorm. Then, when I got his letter I was ecstatic. What causes these intense feelings? Is it love? Really love? I know I love him. But is it the *real* thing? Is it important that I know? I want to see him and be with him. I miss him.

OCTOBER 3, 1980

Bike, take me through this pretty campus. I am so glad that I brought my bike. Five miles a day, everyday, should do it. Keep me fit. After classes on weekdays make myself do it. On the mornings before work make myself. Weekends get up and do it.

I can think. I can feel bad thoughts leave me. They fly out in the wind. My face is flushed. My breath hard. I breathe in life, a life that is and will be special.

OCTOBER 5, 1980

God damn it. What the hell do you think you're doing?

May I have change for a dollar? And another dollar and another? Forty cents will buy you a Snickers. Another forty cents a bag of M&M's. Another forty cents a peanut butter cup. All from an anonymous machine. No one to see you turn red. No one, not even a cashier, to know what you're doing.

You had it made, Miss. Dance, dance, dance. Smile, smile, smile. They see you and they like what they see.

So why again? Why, why, why? It's not the amount anymore. Three bars is not as outrageous as the whole bags of your yesteryears. That's the point: there's no choice. You don't want to, but you do. That's no choice.

Go ahead, be scared. You should be, Beauty.

OCTOBER 7, 1980

I don't want to be misleading. I mean, I don't want to look back on this next year and read about how miserable my life was. Because it's not. Overall, I have been feeling and looking exceptionally well. Almost every day I reflect on the goodness and calmness of my life. I have direction. My page job is wonderful. Life, itself, is wonderful, I think.

I have never been this popular. I could never even have imagined being this popular.

Today, however, and many other times, I feel quite mixed-up. Honestly, *I have come so far.* Just a year ago I had no conception of who I was or what I was capable of. Now I am in college, and I am adjusting. Yet things are missing. Or rather, I am missing home, Perry, etc. I just don't know how I feel. I feel different. As if I am like no one else.

Do I have a lifelong problem with eating? Somehow, I feel the answer is yes. Am I being too subconsciously stringent? What should I do? I love myself and I want to help myself.

OCTOBER 9, 1980

I'm going to take a little trip Friday, Saturday and Sunday. Self-directed. Not a lifetime, just three inner-directed days to get a push. I will not worry about other people. Just me. Just minimal food and maximum exercise. A time to recap and recoup. Walk, jump, dance, run . . . a minute at a time.

Destination: Monday morning.

OCTOBER 27, 1980

If this sounds jumbled it's because that's how my thoughts are. Well, I'm changing again, physically, and, I suppose, mentally and emotionally, too. I've decided that there is more to being thin than being thin. Being thin does not mean being happy, feeling good or even, necessarily, looking good. It takes more. I think for me, it takes eating a *balanced* diet (not just refraining from binging). Plus it takes a fitness program and lots of positive thinking.

My life is so interesting and Perry is the most pleasing part. I guess there's no real way to judge what a true everlasting love is. All I know is that for now I am in love. There really is little question left in my mind.

And he loves me.

There are other boys and men and boys and men and boys. I'm used to it now. Me a heartbreaker, cheerleader, homecoming queen type? That's how people see me.

I seem to be constantly changing. I try to help myself and understand myself in whatever ways I can.

OCTOBER 30, 1980

Perry,

You are a wonderful person.
Whether you realize it or not,
I realize it.
Don't think you are mixed-up. Everyone is confused.
Everyone.
Your mother was right about being able to live.
Let yourself.
Know that nothing you could ever, ever do to me could be wrong.
Don't twist what happens in your mind. It's natural and normal.
Just let it happen.
Then let it be.
Know yourself well enough to know what you want.
Go for it, with no regrets, no guilt.
You are capable of anything.

Lisa

OCTOBER 31, 1980

I can't take this anymore. Up. Down. Up. Down. Is there no inbetween? Where am I?

I am in classes. They are hard (biology, freshman composition, communications, critical graduate cinema), but I am working hard and doing pretty well. Now my cinema professor is telling us we must read German articles (in German!) for our mid-term. Why in hell did I take a graduate cinema course? I didn't know when I enrolled that it was a graduate course, and the description sounded easy. And now the bombs are dropping, and so am I.

I know one thing, with Gary and Rob coming over to study biology (Gary on Tuesdays, Rob on Thursdays), I have changed. Gary is on the baseball team. Rob is Rob, and that's saying a lot. We're all smart, and that doesn't even matter anymore.

The point is, I don't understand myself anymore. I finally thought I had everything that I wanted and I still eat. Not as much and not as often, but they're still binges and I still hate myself when I do it. Why screw up such a wonderful (?) life?

NOVEMBER 1, 1980

"Mom, oh, Mom, please help me." That's what I said today. Finally, I had to tell someone I need help. I can't take it anymore.

I was hysterical in the phone booth. "Mom, I think I heard it's called bulimarexia, but I don't throw up so I don't have that. But there is something wrong with me. I should not be like this. I am ruining my life. I'd rather leave school and fix myself. I can't go on like this. Will you call your doctor and find me a doctor, anyone, to help me?"

I am coming home, Mom. Welcome me back to your arms because I can't take it.

P.S. Don't tell Dad until we have to pay somebody. We'll tell him I'm switching schools next semester because I don't like it here. I'll live at home and go someplace cheaper.

NOVEMBER 2, 1980

I am calmer now.

Tomorrow will be a turning point whether I decide to leave school or stay. Live, love, laugh and *learn*. I am trying to help myself. Why should I make my life miserable by gorging and playing cruel tricks on myself? I told myself yesterday, "If you go out and eat those candy bars while you should be studying for your communications test, you leave the dorm for home immediately. Consequently, you will not study, you will miss a mid-term and you will never be able to come back to school again."

I ate. I went home last night. I missed the mid-term today.

I am a terrific person. Why am I afraid of that terrificness? Why won't I let myself enjoy the benefits of my healthy, trim, serene, beautiful existence?

NOVEMBER 3, 1980

Read between the lines of your life.
You will be amazed at the incongruity.
That which is beneath the surface, is the surface.
Yet it is hidden, repressed.
The spaces between the lines reveal more than the lines themselves.
What are the lines except empty words filling an empty page?
It is what goes on between those lines that is the true essence of your life.

NOVEMBER 5, 1980

FOOD

Breakfast:
    1 slice wheat bread
    1 tbsp. peanut butter
    1 cup non-fat milk
    ½ medium apple

Lunch:
    2 slices wheat bread
    2 oz. roast beef
    1 cup fruit salad
    diet dressing

Later:
    1 large package banana chips
    2 Snickers bars
    2 Baby Ruth bars
    1 large Chunky bar

I've got to cut this out. This is so stupid.

EXERCISE:

Stairs:
    up 3 times
    down 3 times

1 long walk
150 hula hoops

NOVEMBER 6, 1980

The minute I start feeling really good it happens again. I eat and eat and eat to erase the good feeling.

What's wrong? Why won't I let myself be?

NOVEMBER 8, 1980

5:36 P.M.

One minute,
  you wake up
and realize,
  it's time
to take responsibility
  for your life.

5. Limbo

NOVEMBER 8, 1980

What's in store for me? Can I control it? Why did I leave school mid-term? The reasons, I have a feeling, are more complex than I seem to be experiencing. Do I still love myself? Where's that feeling of ecstasy that I had in the summer when I first lost the weight? I want it back. I've got to try. I may not have answers, but I can't give up. No matter what, I'm going to do it. Confidence. That's what I need. I can and will help myself. Ecstasy, here I come.

NOVEMBER 10, 1980

This is the most important thing in my life.

Weight: 120 pounds

FOOD:

Breakfast:
1 diet bread	50
1 tbsp. peanut butter	90
1 cup non-fat milk	80
½ grapefruit	40

Lunch:
1 bagel	140
2 oz. chicken	120

1 apple	40
diet dressing	16

Dinner:
3 oz. bologna	210
12 wheat thins	70

Total Calories	856

EXERCISE:

hula hoops: 400 times
jump ropes: 200 times
jump rope workouts: 2
Richard Simmons on TV
workout: at club

workout: at home
swim at club: 40 laps
bed exercises
bike: 2.5 miles

NOVEMBER 16, 1980

MEASUREMENTS: (My "Live-It" Program Begins)

Waist: 24"

Thighs: 20½"

Bust: 35"

Upper arm: 10"

Hips: 34½"

Lower leg: 12½"

Abdomen: 31½"

Calf: 7"

NOVEMBER 17, 1980

"Live It" Day One
Weight: 115½ pounds

FOOD

Breakfast:
1 wheat bread
1 tbsp. peanut butter
1 cup non-fat milk
½ grapefruit

Lunch:
1 wheat bread
2 oz. turkey
1 glass iced tea

Dinner:
    3 oz. chicken
    ½ baked potato
    mixed veggies
    1 tbsp. soy sauce
    1 tbsp. oil
    1 glass iced tea

EXERCISE

bed exercises	pool exercises
morning routine	evening routine
face-ups	face-ups
hula hoop, 250 times	weights
bike: 1 mile	jump ropes: 100
workout	jump rope workout
swim: 40 laps	

NOVEMBER 17, 1980

Sooo, this is life. Very interesting, confusing stuff. I like myself. A lot. I want to say that first, because I can see that's what it takes. Everything else will follow. I can and will make it. Things won't always be easy, but I think I am learning to cope.

School. I'm really sick of talking about it. What has been done has been done. No regrets. Life and living lie ahead. I'll be working my page job for the next few months and then start broadcasting and journalism classes at Cal State, Northridge. So, I'll get my degree from there. I can't go back to USC after losing all that money and all my scholarships. Well, Perry couldn't believe that I, the straight A student, should drop out my first semester of college. But then, he doesn't know the real reason. I love him, and it's always getting better. I will soon be seeing the psychiatrist recommended through mom's doctor. I think he has a speciality in eating disorders.

Something happened tonight. I'm upset, so everything I say may be regarded as ludicrous and an overreaction later. It's about my father. I don't know if I'm all that wild about him as a person. I love him; he's smart. But I don't like his perspective, where "he's coming from." He called me selfish and irresponsible. It was something to do with the car. He said, "You know, maybe I'll decide Mom needs the car and you won't be able to use it anymore to drive into Hollywood every day for work.'' If only he knew how miserable I am. In one breath he said I could pay him half my savings account and buy the car. In the next he asked why in the world I would give up a deal where I could use a car for free except for gas. If only he knew how miserable I am.

I know what's really important. Keeping my peace of mind. Without it nothing works. I need it in order to live one day at a time.

That's not selfishness. That's survival.

NOVEMBER 19, 1980

Forget this, I am buying the car.

He's, of course, going to say there's no way he said he'd sell it to me for half my bank account. Who'd sell a $7000 car for $1500, he'll ask?

Who'd be stupid enough not to buy a cute little $7000 car for $1500 is what I've been asking myself? Why just drive, in fear of losing your right to drive, when you can own? I'd rather pay repairs and insurance and know that no one can take it away from me.

Later: Well, first he said exactly what I said he would, ''I never said that. That would be ridiculous.'' Then he said he'd think about it. Later he said, ''Yes, if you want to give me half the money in your bank account, I'll sell you the car.''

NOVEMBER 20, 1980

I commit, I commit, I commit.

Others can do it.

I can do it. As one writer put it, I have given up the right to overeat. Binge, that is. I love myself too much. I have faith in me. I am capable of it.

Eating a dessert or treat is not compulsive overeating.

I commit.

NOVEMBER 21, 1980

Perry,

I love you. No point in beating around the bush. Love is not a commitment, but a feeling. The two do not have to go hand in hand.

So don't get scared. I don't want anything from you. I know I seem like an incredibly easy person to please. Maybe I am. It's not that I don't want anything from you, it's just that I'm satisfied with what you feel comfortable in giving.

Giving is not only *things*. That's unimportant and, in the long run, doesn't matter much. People who can give of themselves and share their hopes, dreams, problems and everyday trivialities are the biggest givers.

So I think you're a wonderful person. I think we're both wonderful. Two people who could have anyone they wanted and pick each other. I think that's the healthiest kind of relationship.

I felt like saying it for a long time, but I was afraid. I still am, a little. Over the past months I've seen us both changing and growing. I like the results, but I know we've still got a way to go before we're through.

On what you said about making decisions: I make them. Sometimes they're not verbal, but I would never just go along with something. What I do, I do because I want to. I decided a long time ago, when you love someone, what you do is right.

I just don't want you to feel badly. Sometimes it's hard for me to express myself. Just know that it's more my nature to be passive than aggressive.

Until now I've been playing it safe. There comes a point, though, when you've already given up enough that playing it safe doesn't seem as necessary. I feel relieved.

So now you know how I feel. You probably already did. It calls for no reaction, response or answer.

I'm happy with the way things are right now. I'm happy with you.

(Never Sent)

NOVEMBER 22, 1980

I am a yo-yo. I don't want to be. My life is either terribly up or terribly down. Where is the balance? Where am I? Uncertainty looms. I

don't want to be a yo-yo anymore.
I am grabbing control again.
Live.

NOVEMBER 22, 1980 P.M.

All of a sudden I am very scared. I am a prisoner. I think about it all the time. How I act, how I think, what I do. It is in my every thought. It looms twenty-four hours a day. Every day. Whether I am eating sensibly or overeating, it is always there.

Who am I kidding? I'm not free. I'm locked up. It's always there, either in the front or back of my mind. Controlling me.

What do I do?

DECEMBER 4, 1980

Starting bloated weight: 120½

DECEMBER 5, 1980

All liquid to clean out system and drop water weight.

Dec. 4	Dec. 5	Dec. 6	Dec. 7	Dec. 8	Dec. 9	Dec. 10
120½	119½	117½				

Dec. 11	Dec. 12	Dec. 13	Dec. 14	Dec. 15	Dec. 16	Dec. 17

What It Takes

Balanced low-cal food plan
Exercise
Positive thinking

Ideal Exercise Plan

morning routine
bed exercises
face-ups (2)
100 jump ropes

jump rope workout
200 hula hoops
weights
bike: 1 mile
workout
swim: 30 laps
pool exercises
evening routine

Positive Thinking Plan

Feel good about you.
Think ''up'' thoughts.
Make the most of situations.
Like you.
One day at a time.
Let yourself relax.
Let yourself feel.

DECEMBER 6, 1980

I am all alone.

I am not going back to that guy. I put a message on his service that I was cancelling my next appointment and would not be back. Three times: $300 of my mom's dollars—no dad involved—and he asks me about my infant days. Fine, but every time I'd leave, I'd stop at McDonald's and Jack in the Box and Arby's. By the time I'd get home, I'd be bloated and numb.

This last time did it. He said, you know, Lisa, I notice the few times you've come, you've worn button blouses that buckle a little. He's there looking at my buckling button and asks me if there's anything regarding the size of my breasts and men I'd like to tell him. He hopes he's not embarrassing me, but the thought just occurred to him.

What does this 50 year old plush-officed person know about me and my problems?

As always, I am all alone.

DECEMBER 9, 1980

And so it comes to an end, the year, and another era of self. I guess I should also say a beginning. Honestly, however, I must say that things are not clear.

What does seem clear at this point is that I would like to weigh between 110 and 115 pounds instead of 120 pounds because that is where I look and feel best.

Last summer, after graduation, I lost weight by getting ill and then drinking liquid protein. The weight came off quickly, but when I began eating, what happened? I have to learn to deal with this realistically. Everything is relative.

I need compassion.

I am at a good place.

I love myself. Period. The way I am.

I choose to change.

DECEMBER 21, 1980

I want to write it down so I don't forget. Although I'm sure the best is still yet to come, *wow*, attention from the opposite sex is at a peak. Maybe it's just that for once the attention is coming from very desirable people. Three. All nice looking. In different ways and to varying degrees, handsome, actually. All three are extremely intelligent, again in different ways, and all are extremely interesting/fascinating.

I know I love Perry. I think I'm in love with him. But this experimentation is wonderful.

My first television ''wrap'' party was great! At least I felt great, dancing with stars—TV, music, film stars. And Brent, my until now flirting page friend, is full of passion for me, thinks I'm gorgeous and loves to have me on his arm. Now we've crossed a little over that platonic line. Just take everything slowly.

Thought I was going to tell Greg to get lost and look what happened. Everything's better than ever. I still left the party with him. I think he's sweet and would like to believe he does know about Perry.

Whatever! These sweeties have one thing in common, good taste.

DECEMBER 25, 1980

Turning point. My life is about to begin. I am beginning. Last year about this time I felt as if my life journey was beginning. It was. So what's starting now? The path toward self-honesty. That's different. God, is it going to take work. Day by day. Minute by minute. I can do it. I believe in myself. I really do. I don't have the answers. I never will. But that's part of the excitement; I don't need answers.

All I need is the desire to seek.

DECEMBER 26, 1980

This is a matter of life and death, or more appropriately between living and non-living. Maybe it's not a physical, literal death, but certainly it's an emotional death. I'm binging and purging myself to death.

I opt for life. Every day that option must be renewed. It is not automatic.

I've got it. Right now I'm uncovering and discovering it.

Later

I'm writing this so that next week when I'm feeling good I will not forget how I feel now.

I *feel* fat. I feel ugly. My skin is breaking out. I feel like I look just awful.

This is going to end.

It is. I will.

DECEMBER 27, 1980

I am not going
to forget this
nightmare of a
life.

DECEMBER 30, 1980

So, I learned something. As if I didn't know. The strange thing is that I really didn't. One bite *is* all it takes. God, I really only intended to take one, to prove to myself that I could. I guess if you just don't have that first bite, ever. I'm not just dealing with tomorrow or next week, I'm dealing with my life.

I'm not going to punish myself by not eating, that's just part of the same vicious cycle. In fact, I can use this as a learning experience.

I have a right to my life.

JANUARY 3, 1981

Resolution: to live happily and healthily *and* to be consciously aware of it.

I looked in the mirror. I talked to myself. I watched myself. I saw what others seem to see, a very pretty girl. Why is it that I usually carry a different image in my mind?

I liked what I saw even though it wasn't what I particularly wanted to see. Today wasn't easy, but I took it as it came, and I made it.

JANUARY 7, 1981

Today is January 7, 1981 and I feel wonderful. There is a subtly beautiful feeling tingling just beneath my skin.

The difference, true, is only a few pounds, but it could be hundreds. What causes this shift in moods? A sense of non-being turns to a sense of well-being.

JANUARY 8, 1980

Well, thank God I could get back in. Any student can take up to a one year leave without losing student status. I just registered like nothing happened.

I kept saying to myself these last few months, "Hey, there was a reason you picked this school. You put some thought into this decision. Are you just going to throw it all away?"

I'd be standing on the audience lines at work talking to tourists and they'd ask me where I went to school, and I realized I wanted to say USC. Not any other school, just USC. I finally thought, there's no way I'm going to let this thing eat away my chance at the education of my choice.

So, I'm back. I found an apartment off campus with a girl from Singapore. I like my part of the apartment. It's big. It looks like things might work out after all.

JANUARY 13, 1981

I'm lying in my bed in my room. In my half of the apartment.

So far, so good.

I'm taking things, life, one day at a time.

I can really say that at this moment, right now, I feel happy, pleased.

Way to go.

JANUARY 18, 1981

WEIGHT RECORD (Weekly)

Date:	1/11	1/18	1/25	2/1	2/8
Weight:	120.5	118.5			
Weekly Loss:	_____	2.0			
Total Loss:	_____	2.0			

JANUARY 18, 1981

Waist: 24½''   Hips: 35''

Bust: 35½''   Thighs: 21''

JANUARY 21, 1981

Today is a landmark in my life. Another journey is beginning. I am ready. I am dedicating my life to me by abstinence from compulsive overeating. I have made a commitment to myself. I like myself enough. I am going to take life a minute at a time. It takes what it takes. I am committed to following a balanced eating and exercise program. My life *depends* upon acceptance and execution of these commitments.

I have just closed and locked the door behind me. Ah, the fresh air. The fog makes it impossible to see what lies ahead. It is my life.

JANUARY 22, 1981

I'm 19 and I'm ready to embark. To participate. To live.

Yesterday, I made a commitment. But who am I today? In some ways I don't know. I am pretty. I do have good friends (a list to look back on someday and wonder about): Perry, Noreen, Lisa, Bob, Greg.

I like myself. I wear a size seven.

6. White-Knuckling It

JANUARY 29, 1981

I have reached the point of no return. Abstinence from compulsive overeating is the most important thing in my life, without exception.

My old life is just that, my old life. I will not forget the desperation. However, that is not now, and all that matters is now. Now. It is the present I have given to myself, present moment living.

I realized that my life is my choice. Whether I was consciously aware of it or not, I was choosing to feel miserable.

I do not choose that any longer. I do not need to continue it.

I felt like a snake almost ready to shed an outer skin, a skin that served no purpose and yet was hanging on, still remaining part of my life.

The skin has been shed. The nightmare is over. I can make my life over.

It *is* over, because I choose it to be. I have that power. It has *no* power. I have always had the power. Now I realize that, and I choose to utilize and channel it positively.

JANUARY 29, 1981

Life at last!
''Point of No Return'' Day 1

Breakfast:

1 wheat bread	70
1 tblsp. peanut butter	90
1 cup non-fat milk	90
	250	calories

Lunch:

1 apple	45
1 apple	45
	90	calories

Dinner:

3 oz. chicken	180
½ cup wheat rice	70
vegies	30
12 grapes	40
1 tblsp. soy sauce	30
	350	calories

Total: 690 calories

FEBRUARY 3, 1981

"Point of No Return" Day 6   Weight: 119 pounds

Breakfast:

1 wheat bread	70
1 tblsp. peanut butter	90
1 cup non-fat milk	90
½ grapefruit	40
	290	calories

Lunch:

1 turkey hot dog	100
1 oz, cheese	60
½ sm. potato	70
1 tblsp. diet dressing	25
12 grapes	40
	295	calories

Dinner:

1 oz turkey ham	65
2 oz cheese	140
diet dressing	25
wheat bread	70
cooking oil	20
	320 calories

Total: 905 calories

Later

This is hard, leaving an old way of life for a new one. Remnants of the old keep pulling and beckoning; they are so ingrained. However, all that's left is that ingrained feeling. The reasons for the eating behavior are no longer here, as they were for the past six years! Yes! At least six, maybe even as many as eleven, blocked out.

Minute by minute I am creating a new life for myself. I'm worth it.

FEBRUARY 7, 1981

"Point of No Return" Day 10
English Journal
Saturday, 3:30-3:45 P.M.

I had an experience yesterday. Usually, I would put an adjective before "experience," however, I am confused as to just what that adjective should be. I know that what happened affected me, but I'm not sure whether or not it should have.

A woman's voice on the phone at work asked, "May I leave a message for Greg Butler?" Yes. Of course. I wanted to find out who it was, his mother?

"Just tell him Joanie _____ (I can't remember) called. I'll call him later." Who calls to leave a message like that?

"OK. Anything else?" That's what I wanted to hear, more. I don't want to be left with "Joanie," that doesn't tell me anything.

"Yes, just tell him I love him."

What? I always wondered if there were others. Why shouldn't there have been? I'm on the verge of love with someone else. Why shouldn't some girl be in love with him? And yet, unrealistically, I always thought I was the only one.

I have no right to feel jealous or hurt or betrayed. And yet I do.

It being my job to relay messages, I did. I wondered what to write. I wrote it all. Better that he knows I know. Handing it to him, I couldn't look at him. My heart beat quick. He had to work late, in order, no doubt, to avoid our usual end of work "rap and kiss session."

I'm not sure what or how I feel. It was an experience. Period.

FEBRUARY 8, 1981

"Point of No Return" Day 11
English Journal
Sunday, 9:45-10:00 A.M.

Well, Perry just left again. This time, however, it was different. It wasn't a rushed, "My parents will wonder where I am, ha-ha." No parents. This time we pulled an "all-nighter."

Even though we've never "slept together," we've never slept together, literally, either. For me, it added a whole new dimension. How else would I have found out about those allergy induced snores?

No matter how doubtful I am twenty-seven or twenty-eight days a month, these fifteen hour rendezvous erase those doubts at least for fifteen hours. When near him I feel love. I don't wonder. I don't question. I just experience, and feel like yelling it out, or whispering. I never do.

Those fifteen hours also confirm his love for me, at least in my mind. I can feel it seeping through his skin into mine. And yet he's been gone only minutes, and already I wonder.

I pretended we were on our honeymoon. I pretended this was our life together. Then I stopped pretending. I just floated.

FEBRUARY 8, 1981

English Journal
Sunday, 3:45-4:00P.M.

I always thought there was a moment when life began, a starting point, turning eighteen, attending college, falling in love.

It wasn't until I turned eighteen, attended college and fell in love that I realized the absurdity of my attitude. No outside event can cause a lasting significant change. We can't depend on others or external events to make us happy. These can only enhance an already fulfilled individual. They do not create one.

I think it is true that happiness is "in your own backyard," mental backyard that is. If you can't find it there, you won't find it anywhere. That's why happiness remains elusive to so many people, they search when all they have to do is breathe.

We are never powerless. We are never hopeless. We are always what we choose to be.

FEBRUARY 8, 1981

English Journal
Sunday, 6:15-6:30P.M.

Love is confusing. At least, for me. Although I am still in the midst of my first encounter, I get the impression that this is an aspect of life marked by constant uncertainty, that never gets any easier.

One moment I feel quite sure that I am in love. The next moment I feel quite sure it is just infatuation, quasi-love or some other less intense emotion.

Then there are the times I'm absolutely sure Perry's in love with me. (Whenever we're together.) Most of the time, however, I am convinced that his motives are less than honorable. (Whenever we're apart.)

As soon as things gel and become clear in my mind, something, real or imagined, jolts my confidence back into a cloudy daze.

Oh well. I once read that only the insecure people seek security. I yearn for that security which will make me feel secure in my insecurity.

FEBRUARY 12, 1981

"Point of No Return" Day 14   Weight: 118 pounds

FEBRUARY 13, 1981

"Point of No Return" Day 15

FEBRUARY 14, 1981

"Point of No Return" Day 16
English Journal
Saturday, 9:00-9:15 P.M.

Valentine's Day. I'm sure many people get depressed on this day, the day for love, the day for being with your loved one. You can try and forget the significance of the fourteenth, perhaps, by not looking at the calendar. However, if you're alive and well, it's difficult to totally escape the reminders bombarding you through card stores, radio, television and newspapers.

Anyone lonely to begin with is doomed for an even greater onset of more of the same. Those with broken hearts must feel the pain more acutely.

FEBRUARY 14, 1981

English Journal
Saturday, 9:15-9:30 A.M.

"Without rain there could be no rainbows."

Smile. Open your eyes wide to life. Experience. Breathe.
Give yourself rainbows. Let yourself go.

Close yourself up and you will wither.
Live one day at a time, minute by minute.
Create your own rainbows.

We are our own sunshine.
We can live on our own solar power.
A smile is a ray of sunlight.
Shine on.

FEBRUARY 15, 1981

"Point of No Return" Day 17
English Journal
Sunday, 2:35-2:50 P.M.

Last night. A landmark. A milestone. I denied an urge. *I didn't do it.* I didn't binge. Why? I'm not exactly sure, but I did want it to go down in recorded history.

I am kicking this thing once and for all. A destructive, emotional crutch, a crutch that's breaking apart. Because I'm breaking away.

I can walk.

For the first time I can breathe. Never again to suffocate myself.

FEBRUARY 15, 1981

English Journal
Sunday, 2:55-3:10 P.M.

My Knight in shining armor,
My Prince Charming,
I used to dream of you.
Then I waited for you.
You were handsome.
You were brilliant.
Sweet,
Tender,
Jewish!
I couldn't understand where you were hiding.
I decided you were a figment of my imagination,
But you were here all along.
I didn't recognize you at first.
You have helped me to fulfill my dreams.
I love you.

FEBRUARY 16, 1981

"Point of No Return" Day 18

FEBRUARY 17, 1981

"Point of No Return" Day 19

FEBRUARY 18, 1981

"Point of No Return" Day 20

I have found someone I can talk to. From an ad in the school newspaper I end up with the psychologist I dreamed I could meet. I saw her last month on "Hour Magazine."

Well, I actually dreamed I could meet the patient who was with her. Here was a woman on television talking about *my* problem. Even if I don't throw up, the similarities are too many. I thought, if only I could talk to her, she would understand.

And here I make a call and I get the same psychologist. The ad said group therapy, but it looks like I might meet awhile alone with her. What a difference from the other guy. Immediately, my first time there, I felt warmth and comfort and a *woman* I could relate to and respect.

FEBRUARY 19, 1981

"Point of No Return" Day 21
English Journal
Wednesday, 8:00-8:15 A.M.

Restroom philosophy. This tiny cubicle is the only place of refuge on campus. The library was closed. I am alone. That is neither good nor bad. That is just a feeling of the moment.

These last few days have been the first time I've never had anyone to depend on, but myself. It's scary, yet invigorating. For the most part, I am on my own.

The turn of events with my car problems were anything but pleasant, and yet I managed. Am managing. I did not resort to that serpent crutch. Don't get me wrong. The urge to eat was there. Quite strong. I fought it. I'm not exactly sure how, but I fought it.

FEBRUARY 20, 1981

"Point of No Return" Day 22
English Journal
Friday, 7:00-7:15 P.M.

"Many people
go from one thing
to another
searching for happiness,
but with each new venture
they find themselves
more confused and less happy
until they discover
that what they are
searching for
is inside themselves
and what will make them happy is sharing their
real selves with the ones
they love."
　　　—Anonymous

I am lonely, I think. I don't feel terrific. I thought I would after not binging for so long. I'm tired. I'm not exactly sure what I want. I would like to wake up with a charge. Energy. Zest. Eager and ready to go. I would like to keep my mind clear, filled with positive thoughts. I would like to squeeze joy just by being me. Just from being alone. That would make the times with others more special.

I want to secrete a zest for living.

I have that capacity.

It's a matter of perspective and attitude.

Thought control. Present moment living.

FEBRUARY 21, 1981

"Point of No Return" Day 23
English Journal
Saturday, 10:05-10:20 A.M.

I don't like to complain. But, everybody needs an outlet, and all is not paradise in roommatesville. Listed below are some annoying traits:

Messy
　Her room (she's never unpacked)
　Her part of the kitchen
Dog
　Supposed to be gone weeks ago
　I hate him

Barks every morning when I get up
Goes to bathroom on carpet
I hate him
Makes me uncomfortable
   "Why you up so early"
   "Peanut butter make you fat"
Ignorance/Stupidity
   Not sure if it's because she's foreign or just dumb
Desk lamp on kitchen table
Dog on kitchen table
Rice maker on sink
Never puts away her dishes
Disgusting old food in refrigerator
Trash
Has only key, but never takes in mail
Overall Strangeness

OK, so I got most of it out. Now, unless I am going to take specific action, I'm not going to waste my time on it.

FEBRUARY 21, 1981

English Journal
Saturday, 12:00-12:15 P.M.

Friends are important, providing perspectives, outlets, ears. Sometimes they are taken for granted.

A good friend is like a rare wine, long in the making, growing better and more priceless with time. It's better to sip and savor their company than gulp it down all at once.

Bob is my friend, someone I can talk with, someone who listens. He is a sincere, sweet and sensitive person. Deep and intense. Our friendship was a fluke. A lucky fluke. The first person I met in college. One of the most important.

FEBRUARY 22, 1981

"Point of No Return" Day 24

DAILY FOOD PROGRAM

Breakfast:

1 non-fat milk	90
1 fruit	40
1 bread	70
1 meat	90

Lunch:

Vegetable	40
1 fruit	55
2 breads	140
2 meats	160

Snack:

1 fruit	60

Dinner:

1 non-fat milk	90
vegetable	40
1 fruit	50
1 bread	70
3 meats	240

Total: 1235 calories

NO PEANUT BUTTER.
ONLY ONE OUNCE OF CHEESE PER DAY.
MEASURE THINGS WHEN POSSIBLE.
DO NOT EAT BEEF.
ONLY ONE CAN OF SUGAR FREE SODA PER DAY.
TWO GLASSES OF WATER PER DAY.
DO NOT LEAVE ANYTHING OUT.

FEBRUARY 23-FEBRUARY 26, 1981

"Point of No Return" Day 25
"Point of No Return" Day 26
"Point of No Return" Day 27
"Point of No Return" Day 28

FEBRUARY 27, 1981

"Point of No Return" Day 29

I feel wonderful. Finally. Fitness. Energy. Vitality. This is great. The payoff from not binging.
   I feel better than ever. It's worth it.
   Here's to today and todays.

FEBRUARY 28, 1981

"Point of No Return" Day 30

I am in the process of learning to love my life, to love myself, unconditionally. I have been changing gradually. This has been the most remarkable thing I have done. In ways it's been powerful, in other ways subtle.
   A month of abstinence from compulsive overeating.

I am learning to cope. My mind is clear.
I feel wonderfully terrific.
Spectacular.

English Journal
Saturday, 5:.30-5:45 P.M.

I ate Chinese food today. Big deal? It was! Anything that has to do with controlled eating is a big deal for me. Controlled is the operative word. In the recent past I would have eaten the Chinese and everything else in sight (and out of it, too). Under the guise of having food that I enjoy, I would have set a trap, then the guilt would come, and a binge with it. So what's changed? I have. I still am. I took charge of the situation. Today, I thought it would be nice to have

Chinese food. Not a single ulterior motive. I planned. I took precautions. Since I had a later breakfast I would skip lunch, just have a big apple when I got hungry, then I could have a combo lunch-dinner meal.

No guilt. Well, not really. Some of those old feelings are gnawing just under the surface. However, I know that they are just remnants of a past behavior to be ignored. It's getting easier. It's not easy. I've taken the liberty of writing my own fortune cookie (along with my own ticket):

> You've come a long way, Baby,
> And you're still going strong.

DAY 30 OF ABSTINENCE!

English Journal
Saturday, 5:45-6:00 P.M.

I love my job. I realized this to a greater extent yesterday. After a week of car-induced absence I couldn't wait to get back. Of course, a lot had to do with my renewed vitality. However, I really like what I do. Working at a television station is exciting. It's fun. It's the right place for me to be now. The people, some of them at least, are so nice to be around. I feel like some of my energy comes through them.

It's true, at times, I was getting—I don't know, not bored, not tired—I'm not sure. Not totally thrilled with all the standing. Nothing, however, is totally thrilling all the time. At least, I don't think so. Nothing I have done so far has equaled the overall satisfaction (on a prolonged basis) I have felt at this. Seeing Perry on a consistent basis comes close, however. Well, it's a foot in the door. It's not stuck in there, though. It's just resting comfortably, tapping away to an invigorating beat.

Bulimarexics to receive help
Binge/purge when distressed

By Janet Schrimmer

When the pressures of everyday life get to be too much for Cathy, she laces up her tennis shoes and takes a 30-minute jog. Andrea lights up another cigarette and Bill gets himself another beer.

Sharon has her own method of dealing with stress anxiety, she goes on an eating binge—devouring everything in sight, then she forces herself to vomit it all out.

Sharon's behavior is a form of a

disorder known as bulimarexia.

While bulimarexia has been around for years, the embarrassment felt by victims of the disorder has kept the problem hidden. The disorder is believed to affect tens of thousands of persons and is especially prevalent on college campuses among upper middle class women.

"The bulimarexic is usually a slender or normal weight woman who thinks she is overweight. Most tend to be attractive, well-groomed and very high achievers. There is nothing physical about them that would make you think there was anything wrong with them," said Anita Siegman, a psychologist and director of University Counseling Services, who will be establishing a support group for bulimarexics at the university.

"Food temporarily relieves the anger and depression most of these women feel. When women haven't learned to deal effectively with either of these emotions they may easily turn to food for a solution."

The name bulimarexia is a combination of the words "bulimia" (an insatiable appetite) and "anorexia" (the abnormal rejection of food). While daily patterns vary from bulimarexic to bulimarexic, the binge-purge obsessions are always present. Purging (to rid oneself) is usually done through vomiting, but extreme doses of laxatives are also commonly used.

"Most bulimarexics depend on their families very much, but they also strive to maintain independence. The need for perfection is often present, and that's why you see so many bulimarexics on college campuses. They're high achievers. They're obsessed with being thin and are often the classic 'good girls'.

"They often fear interpersonal intimacy—either on a sexual level or simply on a friendship level," Siegman said. Bulimarexics soon become so preoccupied with their bing-purge ritual that there's little time to develop or maintain relationships.

The purging following a binge, relieves the guilt felt from overeating and prevents a weight gain. Eventually the urge becomes habit forming and a lack of control is established.

"This lack of control is the most frightening thing about the disorder, especially since most of these women have a lot of control in other areas of their life."

Most victims are between the ages of 18 to 25, however cases have been reported among women ages 13 to 60. The disease is extremely rare in men because the relentless pursuit of thinness is not so innate, Siegman said.

They often fear interpersonal intimacy . . .

"This obsession to be thin has become more than a psychological problem. It has become a societal problem especially here in California. Our society sends messages to women that tell them if they can't fit into a size three jean then they haven't made it as a woman no matter what else they have going for them."

"The warmer weather of the West Coast and the additional recreational opportunities have also helped to create this preoccupation with the physical attractiveness of one's body. As a result there is a tremendous amount of pressure felt by women and many have a hard time accepting their bodies," Siegman said.

Siegman, who has counseled several women on an individual basis, plans to start a group which will enable bulimarexics to share experiences and obtain help.

Siegman and Eric Cohen, a Student Health Center physician, have directed several other groups and believe strongly in the notion that a group offers a tremendous amount of support and is a favorable method of obtaining therapy. It also helps participants view others who share a common problem and this helps banish feelings of isolation, Siegmen said.

"The purpose of this group will be to assist women who feel caught in a cycle of binging and purging relative to eating behaviors. Specific techni-ques to control bulimarexia and to put food in perspective in one's total lifestyle will be dealt with in a safe and supportive atmosphere," Siegman said.

The group is scheduled to begin this week and is free of charge to students.

MARCH 1, 1981

"Point of No Return" Day 31

Well, I spoke with the University psychologist who's starting the groups today, and it looks like I'll be part of this first eating disorder group. I have to say, and I told her, I think I'm much better than I was. After all, as I told her, I haven't binged in over a month. Even though this group is popping up at a time when I'm coming out of it, it's the first time I might be able to talk to anyone, let alone people my own age, about this. Maybe I can even help people with my experiences. This, in addition to my weekly sessions with Francine, can only endorse what I've taught myself. I've been alone so long, I can't pass up an opportunity to finally talk.

MARCH 1, 1981

English Journal
Sunday, 11:35-11:50 A.M.
Written in car. While parked.

Writing as preventative medicine. Take it a minute at a time. Don't wonder what Bruce is thinking. Don't even think about the end of the evening until the end of the evening. You know you don't want to get involved romantically with this person. You're both pages and you're friends.

You like him. Period. You want to stay friends. You will. This is not a date. This is just a day with a friend. Big deal. Enjoy it for what it is. Don't take it out of context or blow it out of proportion.

English Journal
Sunday, 12:05-12.20 P.M.

I defended Brent to Greg the other night. It was automatic. Of course, Greg was excedingly paranoid about Brent's feelings toward him. Yet, I had nothing to gain, since Greg is the one I'm going out with, not Brent.

Brent, of course, does a better job as a page than Greg. In addition, he's a very interesting person. Quite nice looking in a sweet, pleasant way. The exterior exudes confidence and humor, but that is only part. He is not always sure of himself. That makes him all the more likeable. He will go far. He'll make it. He's got "it," that special something. Flair. Intelligence. Sincerity.

I like the guy. In fact, sometimes I wonder how much. I was flattered that such a desirable person fell for me. However, I did not want to be put in the position of losing Perry.

I decided, though, that Brent's the second nicest boy (man?) I've ever met. I always thought he put me on a pedestal, which was nice, but not the basis for a relationship. For those few non-platonic days it seemed different, like it could perhaps work. If it weren't for Perry, I would definitely go out with him.

MARCH 2, 1981

English Journal
Monday, 6:30-6:45 P.M.

Well, I bypassed another one. It was not easy. At all. I could see myself eating the whole loaf of bread—in my mind. However, unlike the past, I didn't act on that mental image. I grabbed a diet soda instead.

I still "used" food. However, I added up calories, and decided what I would have beforehand. Eventually, I won't use food at all. I'm doing so much better. I'm really coming around. This was an accomplishment.

MARCH 3, 1981

"Point of No Return" Day 33

MARCH 4, 1981

"Point of No Return Day" 34
English Journal
Wednesday, 1:55-2:10 P.M.

I'm sitting here in a television studio in the midst of a taping. Sister Sledge is singing in the background, later will come Dionne Warwick, Paul Anka, Smokey Robinson, Leo Sayer. And I'm getting paid.

This is my dream job. Sometimes, it has become even blase. But no, deep down and at all times a part of me realizes that this is fantastic. Whether I'm standing for hours, watching a light on a phone, or whatever, I do love it. Not just for the opportunities it offers and will offer, but because it's fun. The people are great. I'm making money. It's a sought after position. Reflecting I realized this is very long for me to stick to an optional activity. It's been eight months with never a thought of quitting.

I'm glad that I'm one of the young ones who will have the opportunity to work here for years.

MARCH 4, 1981

English Journal
Wednesday, 2:10-2:25 P.M.
At Work.

Moving out by myself seems like the best thing to do. It will be exciting. New experiences always are. My own place. She, as a roommate, is intolerable. I'm not perfect, but she really goes too far, and probably doesn't even know it. But I don't want a roommate at all. It's not just her, although she epitomizes the pits of the pits.

I can't explain why I want to be alone; it's just a feeling. Maybe I won't like it. I think I will, and attitude is important.

There are, of course, advantages to living on campus, just as there are advantages to living with a roommate. There are disadvantages in each situation too. All you can do is choose the situation that "seems" to have the most pluses and the least minuses. "Seems" is the operative word. You never know. But that's life, isn't it?

MARCH 4, 1981

English Journal
Wednesday, 2:25-2:40 P.M.
At Work.

A DAY IN THE LIFE . . .

I woke up at 6:15A.M. I had breakfast: 1 egg, 1 piece of french bread, 1 orange, 1 diet coffee milkshake. I made my bed. I exercised. I took a shower. I blew my hair dry. I got dressed. I wore jeans, an alligator sweater and a preppy red shirt. I wore my espadrilles, but one ripped and sent me flying in the garage. I got my stuff together. Put the water bottle out in the hall. Walked down the stairs. Had the shoe incident. Ran back up and changed shoes. Drove to school. Parked. Studied in library. Went to English Comp. at 9:30. Did Eng. exercises. Turned in journal. Ducked in to library study carrel. Ate lunch there. Studied Spanish. Went to philosophy lecture on Plato's morality. Went to car. Had apple. Drove to work. Changed clothes. Went to stage six. Was told to watch the phones.

MARCH 4, 1981

English Journal
Wednesday, 3:30-3:45 P.M.
At Work.

Dear Perry,
This is a letter I'll never send because it tells the way I really feel. We never seem to tell each other that. I'm not complaining, at least that's why I'm not sending it. I don't want you to think that I'm complaining. I don't want to push you away. What I'd like is to be honest, and not have that honesty trigger any effects.

I guess what I really want to know (through mental telepathy, or some other painless method) is how you feel. Of course, this is my insecurity talking. I know that. That's another reason I'm not sending it. It's not a rational request. However, I still feel that way. I'm the type of person who doesn't like to feel I'm wasting my time (or energies), but you're worth wasting my time on, so I just won't ask.

MARCH 5, 1981

"Point of No Return" Day 35

MARCH 7, 1981

~~"Point of No Return" Day~~

Well, I ate and I ruined it.
  Like my life. I'm ruining my life.
  God help me.

7. Momentary Hell

MARCH 22, 1981

The absolute pits. I reached it today. I was totally unable to cope, to function. I never want to be here again.

I can't fit into my page uniform, except squeezed in, and it looks terrible. I've got to do something, foodwise, besides otherwise.

This is a many faceted nightmare. I'm going to search through all this rubbish, straighten up a bit and find myself among the ruins.

MARCH 25, 1981

My first binge after a month of abstinence was a last-ditch effort to hold onto the past, a past that I saw disappearing. My focus has been askew for so long that I was afraid of seeing clearly.

I have so much strength and confidence. I try to make myself forget. I try to push it down. I try to create a false front of weakness, ugliness and inability. The food serves as a hypnotic. Through it I begin to believe and live the false front. And yet, I know that my confidence and strength are locked away and being smothered. Why?

Part of my whole eating problem is that I have not been able to find a balance. I either do everything perfectly, or I do nothing, miserably. Why can't I just live somewhere in the middle? Why do I have to be at the extremes?

MARCH 25, 1981

Before, losing weight equaled feeling good. Now, losing weight equals losing weight. Feeling good equals feeling good. The two are no longer inseparably linked. I am beginning to feel good about myself without any strings attached, i.e., the number on the scale or the amount or kind of food that goes into my body.

In reality, the real reason I should want to lose weight is to feel and look better. The number on the scale really does have nothing to do with that. It doesn't really represent anything.

Oh, how I'll miss my roommate's barbequed grasshopper chile

By Lisa Messinger

"Tushka poopkin farka!" Loosely translated this means, "Save room, we're having baked flies for dessert." Unfortunately, after finishing my moth-head and fish-eye casserole, I couldn't eat another bite.

But don't balk! Just a few short months ago, I, too, would have thought these delicacies unpalatable. However, my diet, as well as my lifestyle, has undergone radical changes since moving in with a foreign roommate.

Don't get me wrong. I'm by no means implying that living with a foreigner can't be a wonderfully enriching experience. And I'd be the first to jump at setting-up housekeeping with Omar Sharif or Mikhail Baryshnikov. It's just that my particular, isolated experience, while it may have been a thrill a minute, was a little too thrilling most of the time.

Of course, there were few benefits. I now know how to say "the toilet's backed-up" and "the dog ate the curtains" in two languages. But let's face it, after paying through the nose for rent, you expect more than a lesson in bilingual complaining.

Speaking of complaining, I didn't do any, I opted, instead for domestic tranquility. That was a mistake. I was driven to the point of raving resentment by not making known my dissatisfaction with my roommate's little idiosyncrasies. At first, I thought ours was just a cultural gap that could be bridged with a little patience and understanding. Believe me, I tried.

I accepted the fact that since animals are believed sacred in her country she couldn't be expected to remove the dog dropping/sacrificial fur shrine that sat atop our kitchen table. Similarly, she couldn't be expected to shut the screens and deny entrance to what she called the "flying gods." Hard as it is to admit, when she wasn't busy praying to them, I secretly shot a few dozen with a squirt of Extra Strength Raid.

Since familial allegiance is next in importance to animal reverence, I couldn't expect her to ask her family to move the campsite they had set up in our living room. In fact, when they were inside the tent, I barely even noticed her four sisters, three

103

brothers, mother, father, two cousins, great-grandmother and a man that, although no one seemed to know, could have been a distant relative.

Good sport that I am, I even submitted (at gun point) to a few family rituals. One night at the campfire, I was bequeathed to her brother. The wedding is set for early June. First, I have to spend three months in basic slave-training.

You're probably wondering, is there no end to my patience? Yes, there is an end. I *can* tolerate almost anything. However, there are some acts so inconsiderate, so irritating, that no apartment co-renter should be forced to put up with. My month's notice has been given because of such an act. You guessed it—she blocked my parking space with her Porsche. Let's face it—there's only so much I can take. I do have to admit, however, I'm going to miss that barbequed grasshopper chili that only she could make.

Lisa Messinger is a freshman majoring in journalism.

MARCH 26—MARCH 31, 1981

"Point of No Return Re-Take" Day 36
"Point of No Return Re-Take" Day 37
"Point of No Return Re-Take" Day 38
"Point of No Return Re-Take" Day 39
"Point of No Return Re-Take" Day 40
"Point of No Return Re-Take" Day 41

MARCH 27, 1981

Dear Perry,
I was going to lie. I was all set to lie. But then I realized that although it's relatively easy for me to lie to other people, I just don't want to lie to you. It would be easier (and from outside appearances more acceptable) to give an excuse (e.g., "I am deathly ill," which is what I was going to say) than it is to even try to give a truthful explanation. However, I'm tired of giving excuses and lying (not to you, just in general.) So, I decided to be honest, especially with someone I love. Yes, I admit it. I love you. (I didn't say I was *in* love with you. There's only so much I can reveal.)

I'm not here. I tried to call you at home and dorm to lie about ruining tonight, but maybe this will be better in the long run. At least I feel like a lead weight is being lifted from my chest. You see, I have been living a double life, like two people. I guess I just can't take it anymore. I don't know why else I would be writing this now.

I have and have had (for eleven years) a problem. It is only recently that I have begun to come to grips with it. And I *am* getting much better.

(Now is the time to read the articles I enclosed, they explain it as well as and less emotionally than I could.)

Bulimarexia
The Binging/Purging Dilemma
By Francine Snyder

Bulimarexia . . . what is it? Although not as fashionable as anorexia nervosa, it is an eating disorder affecting thousands of people. And it is finally out of the bathrom.

Have you heard of compulsive or binge eating? Bulimarexia is characterized by the consumption of large quantities of food. Whole cakes, gallons of ice cream, bags of cookies are often consumed along with large quantities of liquid. Purging follows, and is usually brought about by forced vomiting. Sometimes diuretics and laxatives are used.

The following are typical comments from clients while in the middle of a binge: "I know I am hurting myself, but I don't care." "I don't care if I get cancer from doing this." "I don't care if I die, I just have to get rid of all this food I ate. . . In fact, I wish I were dead." "I can't stand doing this any longer and I can't stand not to do this. The thought of giving it up is just too much for me to bear."

Most bulimarexics learn about vomiting from a parent, friend or relative who has tried the same behavior. The eating and vomiting start out as a lark—it is a way for an individual to literally have his cake and eat it too.

The bulimarexic is generally female and the binging/purging begins sometime around adolescence. It is usually during adolescence that a girl experiences her first rejection. Binging and purging initially solves two problems: It allows her to eat whatever she wants without having to suffer the consequences of a weight gain. And stuffing the food is a great way of avoiding any feelings of anger, hurt or rejection she may be experiencing. Vomiting relieves the stuffed, bloated, uncomfortable feeling the overeating brings about. The behavior becomes obsessive; there is almost nothing that will stop a bulimarexic individual from binging. The cycle is addictive and causes an extreme amount of shame, guilt, isolation and fear of getting caught.

Men are affected by this disorder but to a lesser degree than women. They usually chance upon it after losing weight, when they are besieged with the fear of regaining what they have lost. The binging allows the man to eat whatever he wants and the vomiting enables him to maintain his present weight. In general, there is less social and parental pressure on the male to be "thin." A man is allowed to have more bulk.

For the bulimarexic living alone, the

105

likelihood of someone coming home unexpectedly is not a problem. However, for someone in a relationship or with children, there is the constant fear of getting caught. Imagine the mortification of having just completed a secret binge of a chocolate cake, a half-gallon of vanilla ice cream and a bag of cookies. There you sit amidst empty cartons, torn bags and containers of food, and in walks your spouse. What do you do? What can you say?

Ah, what a relief when you put your children to bed. You are finally alone and can eat and vomit without any distractions. But what happens if the children wake up? Yes, you can tell them you are sick, but how many times can you use that as an excuse?

Noise from the shower may appear to be a great camouflage technique, but what happens when it backfires? What if it wakes someone up, how do you explain running the shower at 2 a.m.?

Then there is the problem of dates and appointments and getting places on time. You leave the office at 5:30 p.m., you make a stop at the 7-11 on the way home. You load up with ice cream, Sara Lee cake, crackers, doughnuts and Cool Whip—and a sandwich so you will have something to eat in the car on the way home. You'd love some peanuts or peanut butter but you know that those foods are too difficult to bring up. As you check out, you make some remark to the cashier about the party you are giving because you would just die if anyone found out about your secret life and that all that food is for you. Then you are off, tearing into the sandwich as you get into the car and mumbling how it's OK to eat the sandwich because you haven't eaten all day.

It's all very exciting and lots of fun. You can eat whatever you want, all those foods you would never allow yourself to eat before because you were always on a diet. Besides, you are extremely health conscious; "Sugar, who me? I never eat sugar. I'm strictly into health foods, fruits, vegetables, tofu. I practice yoga twice a week and work out at the gym at least three times a week." And after all, your friends know how "good" you are. They always tell you how envious they are that you are able to resist the hot fudge sundaes and fresh baked cookies and stay so thin. They all wonder how you can have such incredible willpower. God, what if any of your friends caught you loading up on all this junk food? How would you explain yourself? Oh well, don't worry about that now. You've got your sandwich, doughnuts and cookies; you're OK.

The bulimarexic is usually able to function well at work and is often in a top level executive position. An outsider viewing the typical bulimarexic would probably say the individual has everything she could possibly want. She is likely to have a good figure (average weight or thinner), earn a good salary, have a lot of people around and be extremely competent at her work. She is the kind of person that you admire, respect and perhaps envy.

But there is another side; a side no one sees. The part that is constantly obsessed with food from the moment she wakes up until she falls asleep at night. A great many binge eaters will wake up during the night to eat.

A sample entry in the bulimarexic's journal might read as follows: I get home almost running in the door and stop only long enough to put the grocery bag down. I go over to pull the phone out of the wall while munching on a doughnut. The last thing I want is for the phone to ring. Ah, peace and quiet and tranquility. It's just me and the food. How wonderful! No hassles, no aggravations. No one to bug me. Just peace and quiet and food. What fun!

One hour later — UGH! My stomach is so bloated I can hardly breathe. Ugh, I'd better drink some more water to make sure I will get up all the food. I'd better vomit now. If I wait too long I won't be able to get it all out. Ugh, I can hardly make it to the bathroom. I'm so uncomfortable. My stomach is so bloated. I can't move. This is awful. I can't wait to get some relief, to feel the rush of food as it comes up.

Oh, what a mess, how disgusting. God, I wish I could stop this binge eating. I put my finger down my throat again. What if my friends or business associates saw me now . . . Vice-president of a thriving production agency. What a joke! I feel like a two-headed freak — a Dr. Jekyll/Mr. Hyde. Well, I can't think about it now. I have to concentrate on getting up all the food I ate. Good thing I ate that vanilla ice cream — it comes up so easily.

What time is it? My gosh, it's 7 p.m. I have a date at 8 p.m. I still have to finish vomiting, clean up the bathroom, shower and get dressed. I hope I can make it on time. I've got to keep this up until I've gotten rid of every bit of food I ate and my stomach is completely flat again. Hope my puffy eyes don't give me away. Oh well, John probably won't notice. I hope he won't notice the swollen glands in my neck. I wonder if they would go away if I would stop binging. If only I could stop.

. . . . .

The binging and vomiting is an endless struggle. Once backed into this behavior it is extremely difficult to break the pattern. Some form of counseling or psychotherapy is required to treat the cause, assist in changing the patterns and to teach techniques that will break the binging/purging behavior. Support and encouragement are needed for the bulimarexic who has an addiction that is often as entrenched as the addiction to drugs or alcohol.

As a therapist I view this condition as an opportunity; as a beginning, not an end. It is a time when the individual can turn what has been a negative behavior into a positive learning experience. The food and eating can be viewed in a positive light when it is used symbolically as an aid to the therapeutic process.

Therapy is important to help the clients recognize their needs and learn how to fulfill those needs in a more rewarding manner.

Francine Snyder, R.N., M.A., M.F.C.C., PhD candidate is a psycho-therapist in private practice in Beverly Hills, California. She has been working with people with eating disorders for the last ten years and is completing her doctoral dissertation on bulimarexia.

So, now you know. I don't want you to feel sorry for me. There's no need. Most of the time (some of the time, at least) I'm a pretty confident, "together" person. The woman in the article has been helping me to help myself. And I have been. Just writing this is helping me (it's a big step), and I thank you for being someone I could write it to. So why couldn't I see you? Part of this condition is that we have rules we make ourselves live by. Rules for *everything*. **My** biggest rule has been that if I don't follow all the rules, I cannot see anyone that I want to see. Honestly, I feel like there is no way I could face you (I was literally panicking). I have broken more dates—I hardly will ever let myself see my friends—I've been lonely.

I'm in the process of changing this, but I'm not totally ready yet. And I want to see you. You said you missed me. I missed you a lot, but I'm just not ready yet. When I was going to lie about this weekend I was going to say I could see you next week (but I knew I probably wouldn't feel right about it yet). I do want to see you very much, but I feel like I'd like to wait a few weeks. I can handle the phone, though. I'm not putting pressure on you to call me, and will understand if you don't. To be honest, after this, I'll be scared when I talk to you.

Sometimes I feel envious of you. You seem so well-adjusted, so happy with yourself and your body image, with school, etc. In important ways you're much less inhibited than I, and I'd like to be more like that.

Deep inside I do have a lot of faith in myself, my abilities and my worthiness. It's just that up until now I have put a lot of my energy (and I have a lot of energy) into squelching the confidence and strength that I have. Now that I've realized this, I'm trying to figure out why and change it. A while ago I would never have been able to write this. I would have felt as if I was exposing my whole self and identity, and if it were rejected or misunderstood so would I be. Now, I have it more in perspective. This is only one part of me. It's not all of me. It's not my whole life. I've changed, but I'm still me. And I'm not afraid anymore. I do love you, and it feels good to say it. For me, it doesn't mean anything has to happen, change anything or imply anything. It's just the way I feel.

P.S. Just to keep this honesty bit up, after I decided to write this, I unplugged my phone just in case you got my message. I knew it was important for me to write this, and I thank you for being someone I could write it to. I'd have chickened out if I had talked to you. Please excuse my seemingly strange behavior. But even if you don't, I know it was better for me than lying.

P.S.S. I'll be at my parents' home from now on.

MARCH 30, 1981

Perry: What did she want?!
Joey: To talk to you.
Perry: What about?
Joey: I don't know. We talked for a half hour. You didn't come up much.

Perry: That's encouraging, Joey. Why didn't you tell me yesterday?

Joey: It slipped my mind.

Perry: Terrific, just great. We've got a date tonight, and I want to know why she called! It might be important.

Joey: So call her, Dipshit.

Perry: Yea, I just might do that.

Hmmm . . . no answer. Well, I'm probably worrying about nothing. If it was really important she would have called again. But still . . .

From that moment on a bad feeling overtook my mind and body. A feeling somewhere between anxiety and nausea. A feeling that I tried to get rid of but failed. Two o'clock call, no answer; three, no answer; four, no answer; five, no answer; five thirty, I wanted to call but I was afraid, afraid that you might have been home, and you would've thought it was strange that I was worried that you might not be able to go out. And I was afraid that you wouldn't be there to answer, and I would know for sure you weren't going out with me. So I didn't call. I went in the shower, blow-dried my hair, brushed my teeth, got dressed, finalized my plans for the evening, drove to the gas station, and then, finally, I arrived at your apartment at seven thirty on the dot.

The idea that you would stand me up seemed completely ridiculous, at least that's what I told myself.

"She wouldn't do that tonight. We've been planning this night for weeks. It's just impossible." So in that frame of mind, but still that nagging feeling underlining my confident talk, I jumped out of the car and ran up the steps all set to press #207.

"Oh shit! What's this 'Perry Schwartz' thing?" I tore open the envelope, read the first two pages of your letter, and quickly decided that I had better retreat to the safe confines of the car before I did something rash, like screaming.

There it all was in black and white and Xerox, and I could scarcely believe it was true. I kept looking up at your balcony half hoping I would catch you smiling as if this were some elaborate practical joke. But this was no joke. My fears had been confirmed, and I had the sensation of being almost, well, relieved.

Why should I feel relieved? I asked myself. For one thing, all the tension that I had built up in anticipation of the evening had been released (although not in the way I should have liked!!!). And, moreover, you not being there freed me to do other things. (Like dine at "Jack in the Box" and take in a film by myself.) But there was one problem: Your problem. If it was hard for me to believe that you weren't there, it was even harder for me your reason why!

It all seemed so fantastic. BULIMAREXIA. The infamous Roman technique of gluttony. I could not understand how you could consider yourself a Bulimarexic. I don't think you are. You don't purge yourself by vomiting, so you aren't really. Did you really eat junk food secretly and in vast amounts? I can't envision it! But it would certainly go some way in explaining your meager eating habits that I have seen. When did you come to the conclusion that you were a Bulimarexic and how? Why did it make you develop a rule that never existed before? I am really confused. Do you have to punish yourself to improve? It doesn't seem reasonable.

Another thing you wrote disturbed me. You should not envy me or anyone else. Just as you appear very "together" but have problems, so do we all. I am sure I have just as many personality and confidence difficulties as you. For example, every time I develop the notion that I am good, great, studly, cute, nice, smart, handsome, or just okay, I immediately tell myself I'm a jerk and an asshole (sometimes too loudly!). This is just my way of keeping my ego in check and improving myself. So you see I'm not always the confident, self-assured individual you seem to think I am. In fact, my way of controlling my ego frequently succeeds so well as to make me fear risking anything that might be personally embarrassing. (Why do you think I never asked you out on a date before you asked me?!) You should not envy anyone, least of all *this* jerk writing this.

Lisa, if what you wrote is true, and I have my doubts, I wish that you will succeed in correcting your problem straight away. I want to see you and talk to you (but the phone is too much for me this week). I am still numb from Saturday night. The movies by yourself, and making up stories about what you did the night before, is not my idea of fun. I had and still have other ideas, ideas that include I hope, *you.*

Soon, I hope. Love,
Perry

8. Weekly Therapy: Ah, the Revelations

APRIL 11, 1981

English Journal
5:05-5:20 P.M

Shit! Perry is just like Dad. I picked a boy just like him. One who will never tell me he loves me. And that's what I really want to hear, isn't it? I can give a lot of bull about how it doesn't matter, he ''shows'' it when he looks at me, touches me, caresses me. But still, deep down, if he really does love me why doesn't he tell me so? Once. I feel unloveable. But it's a conflict. I feel like I should be loveable, but I'm not. I'd still be surprised if he told me he loved me. Even though deep down that's what I tell myself is true. Who am I talking about now? Initially, Perry, but it could be either.

I don't know what this means or what, if anything, to do. But it's there, a piece to a puzzle, a puzzle I didn't even know existed.

APRIL 15, 1981

English Journal
11:15-11:30 A.M.

Something hit me the other day, like a ton of bricks so to speak. It is silly, not to mention stupid, to do things now and have the future be your main motivator. What a waste. Now is all the time that is real. I don't want to throw it away.

Take Perry, for instance (anytime, anywhere). I came close to falling into foolhood. How do I know what the future will hold? For some reason, I was not thoroughly enjoying the time we have now in order to placate some future time. Ridiculous. Who knows? We may not end up with each other. For life. But we do have now, or whatever time we spend together.

When he said he very well might join ROTC, go into the Air Force or immigrate to Israel someday, not quite panic, but a scary feeling, an empty numbness came over me. It was hard enough, this being the first time we saw each other since my letter, without having to hear this kind of stuff. It's the first time the future didn't seem quite set. What if our lifestyles and dreams are completely, irrevocably, out of sync? We look at lots of things from different viewpoints. He's very righteous and idealistic.

So, I said, for once, don't think, worry or plan about the future. Just relax and enjoy right now. Learn from and experience right now. It was a nice change of pace.

APRIL 15, 1981

English Journal
3:10-3:25 P.M.

I don't feel very good. What should I do? How should I do it? I don't feel guilty about the sexual feelings anymore. With Greg the other night, I've never been in that position before. He seems so blase. Deep down I wanted to turn him on, and I did more than ever. But not enough. I've never been in the role of seductress or initiator before. Of course, he initiated it as always. But I'm the one who puts my body close against his.

And, finally, he used his hand, but not long enough. I wanted to lead him over to the couch and lie down. But didn't. Why did I feel this way? Maybe it's because he seems so mildly interested. It's not that I'm even thrilled to death while it's happening, although last time I did get turned on when he was pulling me closer.

I do find him sexy and extremely attractive. Perry and he are total opposites, sexually, at least. It was as if Greg wanted to be kissed, but I'm used to being the one who gets kissed and etc. Well, it's teaching me something.

APRIL 16, 1981

English Journal
9:20-9:35 A.M.

Why is it that nothing has ever counted unless I told my parents? It didn't matter that I talked to or went out with Perry unless they knew. I had to subtly let them know that Greg had been here on Saturday. I can't be getting better in bulimia counseling or my group therapy unless they know the progress. Grades don't matter unless they know. It's not just enough that I know. What's the big deal if I know? Sometimes I try to just keep it to myself. But I never do. I always end up telling them in one way or another.

It's as if I am trying to prove something to them. It dawned on me that I'm putting too much importance on what others think and not enough on how I feel, then I feel resentful over that and end up eating. I know what's right for me. I know if I'm in sync. I don't want to have to look to others or put others ahead of me when it comes to defining ME.

APRIL 17, 1981

HEAD: Men Make the *Strangest* Bedfellows!
BYLINE: Lisa Messinger; Sophomore, Broadcast Journalism
425 Words

I've done it on a water bed. I've done it on a twin bed. I've done it on a kingsize. I've done it on a queensize. I've done it in a sleeping bag. I've even done it on a cot. Call me naive. Call me out of it. Call me a virtual ignoramus. But I just don't see what the big deal is. It seems to me that one of the most overrated, overemphasized of our American pastimes has got to be going to bed with someone.

Maybe it's me. I know that after my friends have slept with someone they often feel as though they've had an exhilarating, sometimes thrilling and once in a while spine-chilling experience. Not me.

Why is this? It's certainly not for lack of trying. My quest began when I was still a bright-eyed prepubescent. An idealistic romantic at heart, I decided to sleep only with someone who I loved and, more importantly, loved me: Greggy Pinsk. Greggy Pinsk was my first heart-throb not to mention bedfellow. We had been planning our rendezvous for weeks. It was at the joint Brownie/Cub Scout campout and nature awareness retreat. When our night finally arrived, we sneaked away from the campsite with sleeping bags in hand and dreams in heart.

I became quickly disenchanted, however. The most thrilling sensation I experienced was catching my finger in the zipper when we were zipping our sleeping bags together. After that, it was all downhill. I was awakened by the pine needles puncturing my derriere, the caterpillar crawling up my nose and the dew covering my entire body. It was then that I began to wonder what all the fuss was about.

One of my more recent ventures left me just as bewildered. Being a young college co-ed, I was living in my own off-campus apartment complete with termites and lumpy sofa bed. Buzz Giblet was my current flame. When I kissed Buzz and saw rockets, I felt a renewed sense of hope. However, when I realized that this was just the space shuttle blasting off on television I also realized that there was no real hope for me. I was right. Throughout the night Buzz snored, sneezed, burped and made a number of less identifiable noises. He tossed and turned and in the process kicked me in the face with his workboot. I lost two teeth and any further desire to sleep with anyone ever again.

With this decision came another one: I'll be joining the convent next month. While I may be the first Jewish nun, it certainly seems to beat the alternative.

# # #

APRIL 17, 1981

English Journal
5:00-5:15 P.M.

I'm an "ex." I used to do it. I don't do it anymore. It's a part of the past. Since I am not doing it now, it's a part of my past. I never have to do it again. That activity and mode of self-expression is now over. Yes, over. Gone. No more. I have stopped. I am clean, straight. It's past tense. On April 16, 1981 peace was declared.

Not ignorant enough to believe that discontinuing the activity is the road to happiness. No more. This is a complex issue. To be dealt with. I realize now that this was a catchall for every problem. What do I really want? What do I really need?

There are things about myself that I didn't realize. That I was eating in response to. No more. At least the eating part. I'll have to look at the other part. And that takes guts.

APRIL 17, 1981

English Journal
5:15-5:30 P.M.

I have been dissociating. Put hair spray on my hair. Hair looked good.
Put hair spray on again. Same result. Therefore, hair spray equals pretty hair. I lost touch with what my hair really looked like. All that
mattered was that the hair spray was on. Then the hair must look
good, right? Looking good, too. Make-up had to go on a certain way.
Exactly. Then I look good, right?

If I put only certain quantities of food into my body and exercise it
x number of times exactly, then that makes it look good too. If I don't
do this stuff, there is no way I can look good. I had really stopped
looking at myself. It's easier to just do x and get y than have to deal
with an unknown.

Last night I couldn't believe that I looked pretty, my face, even
though I wasn't eating well. How can this be? It doesn't follow. Or
does it?

Wake up! Be realistic. Your mind has been playing tricks on you.
That was my way of life: Do this and this and this and you get this.
Sometimes that may be true, but not all the time. So what are you going to do? Well, of course, realization is a crucial first step. I'm going
to try and identify it in my life. I've got to learn to live with myself
on a much less rigid basis.

APRIL 20, 1981

English Journal
10:40-10:55 A.M.

I don't want to be around people. I don't want people to look at me.
Why? It's simple. I don't want to look at myself. I asked myself, if I
never had to see anyone, ever, would I still care how I looked? Maybe
not. However, I would probably care how I felt, if I was sick or
healthy. If you're fat, you feel differently, unhealthy. So, I would care.
I used to be able to say, to hell with what *they* think. I know I'm
good, and that's all that matters. I don't do that now because I don't
have that same feeling of self-validation. If I did, I'd say to hell with
them.

I like looking good. It gives me satisfaction. I don't feel I look good now. I don't do it as much for others as I do it for my own sense of accomplishment and progress. I do it to feel good about myself.

I've learned that there's more to me, though. More that has to be dealt with and felt good about. Okay. Fine. But that doesn't mean I shouldn't care about how I look. It's important to me. I've been letting it slide. A lot. One hundred twenty-eight pounds!! And I don't feel good about that part of myself because of it.

I don't want to get fanatical. I don't want to punish myself. God, I'm not punishing myself. I'm just taking Easy Street.

If I could lose weight as fast by eating, I would. I wouldn't not eat to punish myself. So there. One back-of-the-mind theory smashed.

I don't like being overweight. So, I will lose weight. Just because I've stopped binging doesn't mean that I understood why I did it in the first place. First, it's a cover-up. Second, it's a habit.

So, I'll try and figure out what it's covering up. Plus, use behavior modification to break the habit part.

APRIL 20, 1981

English Journal
11:00-11:15 A.M.

Sex. What does it mean to me? This may also be one of the cover-ups. If I had what I thought was a terrific body, I'd want to flash it around. Maybe. I guess I don't want to have to deal with that. If I don't like my body, I don't have to see anyone and, therefore, don't have to worry.

I never admitted I had sexual feelings and desires. That I like it. Who me? Yes, under the right circumstances. Which are? Me. Looking and feeling terrific. That's what scares me: If I feel comfortable enough with me, I may not wait around for Prince Charming (or Perry Schwartz, for that matter). I know it's normal to have sexual feelings, but it's easier not to make any decisions. I don't feel sexual at all when I don't like how I look. But I know if I liked how I looked then I would feel sexual. Of course, I wouldn't even kiss just anyone. However, I know I'd be more curious than I am now. Like Greg, for instance, we know each other so well. We're more than platonic. If I felt more confident, I'd like to go further with him.

And I know I'd be more relaxed with Perry. I'd be able to be the one to start something instead of just lying there like a dead fish. Why am I scared of this? What can I do?

APRIL 20, 1981

This little place. This little studio. At least it's mine, mine alone. Fifteen minutes from campus. Miles and miles from home. Fully furnished (yuk). It's mine. I still have that need to be alone. No roommate. No dorm-mates. No family. God, for the week and a half I was there after I gave Perry my letter, I felt like I was under guard. Eyes on me at all times. I told my mom, but that was it. I felt jumpy every minute, like they were thinking I was going to drop out of school again. All the money down the drain again. At least that's what I felt from my dad who barely spoke to me. Every night I just went right up to my room after I got home from school. Sitting down in the living room with them, I felt like I might jump out of my skin. I couldn't talk. I felt like I might cry or explode.

Well, here I am, just me. Me, just me, and my thoughts.

APRIL 20, 1981

English Journal
10:45-11:00 P.M.

Tomorrow I start the 7-day Philippine quick weight loss reducing program. Well, I start the preliminary two day fruit juice cleansing fast.

I think I can fast for two days knowing that on the third day I can have some of that balanced good food I bought. Thirty-six dollars worth! It looks balanced and filling and interesting. And you can lose between ten and fifteen pounds in that reducing week.

I didn't want to go back to my old balanced eating. Even though I could have lost weight. I wanted an easy way to lose this fat which is not me! That was too slow. I would stop eating nutritiously and then just end up gorging. It was not working.

This is a compromise. I can eat healthily and be full and still lose weight quickly.

As for keeping it off, I may like it enough to expand on it. Or if I go back to my 1000-1200 calorie plan that should maintain it.

Omitting, of course, binging. I have to deal with that. But I'm not going to be able to if I feel like I'm fat.

When I feel better about how I look, I think I'll be less driven and

117

have a better perspective.

APRIL 21, 1981

English Journal
6:15-6:30 P.M.

A nice-looking stranger just said hi to me. What is it that happens
when I feel in control? Because I'm certainly not skinny, just as when
I thought I was fat, I wasn't. What is it? I'm sitting here (College
Library) drinking strawberry nectar.

Dawned on me, I eat to cop out. If I didn't demand such rigidity
from myself then I wouldn't need to cop out. I could just plain live,
experience and enjoy.

How? Well, one way to start is to listen and follow my inner
signals. About work. Trust myself. I'll do it. Twenty-four hours is
enough time. I want to trust myself and give myself more leeway.

I'm a good kid. And besides, sometimes I like to be "doing." I'm
really not lazy. But I do need time to relax, rest and be leisurely. I
have to give this to myself.

Listen and Trust.

APRIL 22, 1981

"INVENTORY"

Eight pieces of wheat bread with margarine (afternoon)

Ralphs: (late P.M.) $7.40
   granola clusters (box)
   granola bars (box)
   diet ice cream (quart)
   diet candy (box)

Burger King: (later P.M.) $7.50
   1 Whopper with cheese
   1 chicken sandwich
   1 ham and cheese sandwich
   2 small cokes/1 small Dr. Pepper
   large fries/onion rings

(Monday, Chinese Food; $7.50)

APRIL 22, 1981

Lisa Messinger
Philosophy 100

> If our actions are not completely under our
> control, are we morally responsible for them?

YAHTZEE!! I feel as though I have scored an emotional and unexpected Yahtzee. The dice that I threw, however, represent more than just the plastic playing pieces of a cardboard game. They signify facets of my life; and they have finally come together. It is as if I have been trapped in a mental Yahtzee game. I knew the straights, full houses, doubles and triples. I was not, however, consciously aware of the importance, or even the existence, of a Yahtzee roll. With hindsight, though, I can look back and see that it was an unconscious desire for that very Yahtzee that motivated many of my actions.

I am referring analogously to my six year bout with bulimarexia, the binging-purging eating disorder. I thought I knew why I chose this behavior. I thought it was a conscious choice, one of my own free will. Recently, however, with the help of a therapist, I realized this was not the case. My motivator has actually been feelings and desires that I had repressed. The fact that I had felt unloved by my father was something I never, ever admitted to myself on a conscious level. Yet, now it seems clear that that has been what prompted some of my bulimarexic actions. I was surprised and confused. If my actions were not completely under my control, not completely free according to philosophical definition, was I still responsible, morally or otherwise, for what I had done to myself? After careful deliberation, I feel the answer is yes. I examined both my unconscious motivations, which I did not have control over and the conscious actions that they led to, which I did have control over. I conclude that any tangible results, those which I would be responsible for or not responsible for, occurred directly because of my conscious actions regardless of what my subliminal motivations may have been. Although this is only one case, the logic used can be applied to other instances where responsibility is questionable.

So far, I have stated that unconsciously I was unfree. It is necessary to examine this more carefully, however. For, if I were both conscious-

119

ly and unconsciously free then there would be no question as to my responsibility. However, my unconscious behavior does not coincide with definitions of freedom. If we use Harry G. Frankfurt's conclusive definition in ''Freedom of the Will and the Concept of a Person'' as a base, my conduct appears to be unfree. Frankfurt contends that an act, A, is free if and only if it was caused by a desire to do A such that one, the agent wanted to act upon the desire to do A more than any other desire he had at the time; and two, his priorities were shaped by reason and awareness and with a sensibility to the consequences. Let A equal my action, which was eating. The agent, me, did *not* want to act upon the desire to do A more than any other desire I had at the time. On the contrary. Action A was merely a substitute for my real desire, to feel loved. I convinced myself that my top priority was to eat when it was not. As a result, my priorities were not shaped by reason and awareness and certainly not with a regard for the consequences. Since I was not fulfilling my top priority, a need for love, the consequence would inevitably be more eating in an attempt to fulfill this desire. But since I was unaware of this desire in the first place, I could have no idea as to the consequences. My priorities, therefore, were shaped by deception and fear and were consequently unfree.

However, it is precisely because of this deception that I can say that I am responsible for all of the results of this destructive eating pattern. Because of this unconscious delusion, my conscious action, eating, can be seen as a free action. When I actually ate, I was in accordance with Frankfurt's definition of freedom. On a conscious level, I had one desire that topped all others: the desire to put food into my body. This was not only a strong desire, it was a priority. I also had other desires. I wanted to lose weight, but I wanted to eat more. I wanted to do homework, but I wanted to eat more. I even wanted not to binge, but I wanted to binge more. I was also aware of what I was doing. I was breaking my personal code. I was doing something wrong, I knew this. I was also very good at employing reason: I need this for energy; I didn't eat yesterday, so there's no harm in gorging today; peanut butter is not a solid food. I also had the consequences in mind: I would gain weight; I would be disgusted with myself; I would probably do it again or starve as a result. Consciously, therefore, according to Frankfurt, I was free.

A single action, therefore, can be unfree in some respects and free in other respects. The question we are concerned with here is which respect deals with the aftereffects, the tangible results. Needless to say, if it were the unfree aspect that led to the results, the agent should not be held responsible. On the other hand, if it were the free aspect that led to these results then the agent could be held responsible. In my case there is a disguised action and a clear action. The disguised action is an unconscious attempt to block out feelings of being unloved by filling or masking the gap with food. The clear action is the conscious eating for superficial reasons. The results of the disguised action are inconclusive. I do not get love; but this is not negative since I didn't know I wanted it. The results of the action, eating, however, are recognizable, weight gain and disgust. These are the results of bulimarexia that I would either be responsible for or not responsible for. These are results of the free aspect of the action. Therefore, I am responsible for these results.

Although this may seem isolated, it can be applied to other cases. People often delude themselves. Therefore, unconsciously, because they do not know their true desires, they are unfree. Consciously, however, they do know what they are doing, although it may be for misguided reasons, as a result of their delusion. They are consequently free in this respect. Even though they are under a delusion, they are aware of the impending results. Therefore, although they are not totally free, they are, nevertheless, responsible for these consequences.

APRIL 23, 1981

English Journal
6:20-6:35 P.M.

I don't think of other people as seeing me as a person. Now I understand better why I avoid people and eat instead of dealing with them. I feel like they only see me by how I look and what I do, not what I am. Maybe it's because I've judged myself that way a lot. If I do good and look good I don't have to look inside. Is it related to Dad? Do I feel that he doesn't know or wouldn't like me as a person. He just knows my accomplishments and the outer crust, how I look. He doesn't know the rest. How do I change this view I have? What do I do?

I asked myself, if I were alone on a desert island, would I care about how I looked? First I thought, well, there's no reason for it, but, then I realized that I would care about how I physically felt. The shape you're in and the food you eat have to do with this, but it's not how you look. So, my desire now is more to feel good.

Most of the time when I eat it's to "cop out" of something. Maybe I put too much pressure on myself, do expect perfection, and if

I would relax and listen, really listen to myself, I wouldn't want or feel a need to cop out.

There is no future for Perry and me. We don't want the same kind of lives. And I don't want him (if I could have him). I never think it, but I don't like our relationship now. I clung to the idea of "someday." There is no someday. There is no now. It's over.

APRIL 23, 1981

English Journal
11:00-11:15 P.M.

Could it be that all the dieting, rigidity of exercise, etc. is a cover-up? Since I binge, I have to do that to be okay. In my mind that's the only way I could ever be okay, right? Why, why is it just me? There must be people who are thin who just eat and moderately exercise whenever they want. It seems so incomprehensible to me to picture a life where I would just live and not follow a definite plan. I never questioned my structure before.

Maybe it would just happen if I let it. Maybe it's what I thought, because I expect such rigid adherence to these plans, I can't do it, so I have to "cop out." IRONY. I make the plan in the first place to stop, refrain from, and forbid the eating and then it's this very plan that causes me to turn to eating. I'm tearing now. I think I've really hit something.

This is scary because it pulls the whole rug out from my way of life. I never questioned my methods. I never knew why I couldn't follow them.

Maybe I don't need a plan like that. The time I stopped binging it seemed like things just started happening. I felt like I was losing weight without "willing" it to happen. Lately, I've realized I've made my life a prison sentence. Do this now. Do this next. Do this. Do this. What should I do? Now I feel lost.

I was making myself diet. I was making myself exercise. It was not directly because I wanted to feel good, or felt like it, or for any really rational reasons. I was (am) doing it because I *had to*. Why is that? I want to eat and exercise when I want to and for a reason. In the back of my mind I knew what I was doing didn't make any sense. I was putting so much true energy into the diet and exercise for what I thought were obvious reasons, to lose weight and look good, and yet I was putting just as much energy into frenzied eating. I knew the two were cancelling each other out. And didn't fit. Somehow I feel that if I stop the binging I won't need that superhuman effort in order to feel good or look okay. Eventually I just would. That spells relief with a capital "R." But is it true?

APRIL 24, 1981

Well, the lid has finally blown off. The cover is blown. It's all out in the open now. All the blood and guts are on the floor.

Well, Dad already knew. I mean we had to tell him in order to afford Francine every week. I didn't go into much detail. It was hard enough to tell something to someone you know won't understand in order to get money. And, by all appearances, he didn't understand. He'd never heard of it.

"I sometimes eat 5 or 10 cookies after dinner, even if I'm on a diet, and I feel bad," he said. "But I stop. Why don't you just stop yourself. So, you've got a sweet tooth."

Sweet tooth. I'll show you sweet tooth. When they came over today, after my crying conversation on the phone with my mom that my dad did not love me, I knew I was finally ready to say something. I couldn't stand it anymore. I realized a big part of my problem, it was trapped in me and it had to come out.

So when my dad antagonized me by saying again how when he saw ice cream cartons or cookie boxes under my bed at home he thought I just had a sweet tooth and didn't want anyone to know about it, and besides, I was always so touchy and preoccupied with my looks, and always going up to my room when I was living at home growing up, he just didn't want to upset me by bringing it up.

"Upset me!" I said, "you want to see what a sweet tooth I have?" I hadn't thrown out the trash of yesterday's binge. I happened to have it hidden in the closet in a shopping bag: a medium pizza box, a bag of potato chips, a pint of ice cream, candy wrappers, junk food cartons. This is not just a sweet tooth, I kept yelling.

"Okay, okay," he said. "I can see that."

I'm sorry I made my mom hysterical. Although I wasn't too far from hysteria myself. "We'd love you no matter what, no matter what," she kept crying.

When I said I thought he wouldn't love me no matter what, he said, "You and Robert are the most important things in the world to me." *Things?*

"But you wouldn't love me, I feel, unless I look perfect and do perfect in school," I said.

"That's ridiculous," he said.

"You wouldn't love me no matter what," I said.

Ah, the zinger. The $64,000 question.

"How can I write you a blank check for my love?"

"Oh, my God." (Mom)

"What do you mean?" (Me)

"What if a kid robbed a bank or was a mass murderer and went to the electric chair? How do you love them then?" he said.

"Oh, my God, I'd love my child no matter what they did." (Mom)

"I'm not talking about *anyone*, I'm talking about me," I said. "You've known me for 19 years, you can't bet yet that I won't be a killer or a criminal. I'm talking about *me*."

"Still, how can anyone write a blank check with love?"

"Don't you see you're telling me there's a line I can't cross over? I don't know where it is. I believe that line to be not getting straight A's or looking perfect."

"That's ridiculous."

"Why? You say you wouldn't love me no matter what. How am I supposed to know where the line is drawn?"

"How can you say that to her?" (Mom)

"So you can't tell me that there's nothing *I* could do in my life, the life you already know, that wouldn't make you stop loving me?"

Increduously, "You can't tell her you know her well enough to know you'll always love her?"

"I guess so."

We brought dinner in and ate. He said, "You won't need this (shopping bag) anymore, will you?" And threw it out.

So, what can I say? In a way, I'm relieved. I am not crazy. I was *right*. I had a parent who did feel the way I thought he did. I thought, how could my feelings be right? And yet, now I see, to some degree, I was right. That gives, I suppose, some validity to the disgusting actions that have been masking all these years the way I really felt. Of course, this can't be the sole explanation. There must be other reasons, too. But, nevertheless, I feel as though a brick is off my head.

I've upset my whole family. The family I've tried so hard not to upset before. I wasn't crazy.

APRIL 25, 1981

English Journal
6:00-6:15 P.M.

About Perry. It is so confusing to me that I could have been doing things—seemingly important things—without ever truly questioning my motives, or if it's the best thing to do.

Without really admitting it, I thought I wanted this relationship for the "future." We were waiting for something to happen. That's why I had to "settle" for now, and eat and eat and eat to push down my real feelings. However, I never even thought honestly or deeply about whether or not I even wanted a future with him. I just assumed, "He's certainly good enough. He's probably it."

But he's not what I want. I do like him right now, at this point in time, but not for the long run. We don't want the same things out of life. He also seems so condescending without even trying to be. Like he'll put up with my "kooky" eating behavior. Well, gee, thanks. I don't want to be put up with. I want to be loved, accepted and understood.

And I don't really like his snobbishness around other people, his righteousness or his highly moral attitude. He's narrow-minded. I think that's sad.

I want more than he is. There is no future. There is no now. Perry and Lisa are coming to an end.

APRIL 27, 1981

Messinger
Too Young To Die
1-1-1-1

Sarah was a friend of mine. Not a close friend. But close enough for me to know that her recent suicide was a mistake. Some might say that suicide is always a mistake. Maybe. This one was.

Sarah thought she knew everything. She didn't. She was sure there was nothing "out there" for her. She was wrong. She was a high school senior. She didn't know there was life after high school graduation or, for that matter, after college graduation or marriage or med school or thirty.

Sarah, if you can hear me, there's something I'd like to say. If you can't, maybe someone else will. If no one should hear, I will. I'll learn to appreciate my own problematic existence, because life can always change.

Sarah, you did it at the wrong time. It was such a waste, because you didn't know. You just didn't know. Life isn't high school, Sarah. Far from it. Of course, while we're there, it's hard to realize that there's more. That it's better. That it's different. But it is. If only you would have let yourself find out.

Why couldn't you have waited? Why did you think that you had all the answers? Answers that you felt couldn't or wouldn't solve your problems. Why couldn't you have waited and found out that sometimes problems just seem to pass away with time? And when they don't, nothing is insurmountable, Sarah. Nothing!

I know you think that I think your problems didn't go beyond broken prom dates, perennial second places and unfinished term papers. You're wrong. I know. Oh, I don't know exactly. But I do know that your disturbances went much deeper.

But, Sarah, what leaves me so incredibly angry and empty is that had you waited, you would have probably discovered something, growing up brings with it strength. Your problems may not have gone away, but you would have fought them or, at least, accepted them. I know you would have.

Just as I know that you, Sarah, the perennial people pleaser would have eventually become your own person. One day you would have woken up and known that your own opinion was more important than that of your parents, than that of your friends, than that of anyone. You would have realized that you alone control your life. And, Sarah, at that moment you would have grabbed control. You would have come alive.

Sarah, why the hell did you have to be so intelligent and mature? I see it in so many mature and intelligent people; you think you know it all. You may know a lot, but *nobody* knows it all. Your world may have been falling apart yesterday. It may be rotten today. But as for tomorrow, next week or next month, who's to say?

Sarah, I have to say it, you were so damned ignorant. I know. I felt miserable through most of high school, too. Now I can see that my vision was terribly limited, almost blinded. I would never have guessed that only months later, I would have a dream job, totally new friends and, most importantly, a completely revised and more realistic image of myself.

I have come full circle, Sarah. Unfortunately, you circumvented yourself. I didn't know what was in store for me. It just happened.

You thought you knew what was in store for you. It's too bad that you were wrong. Too bad and too late.

MAY 1, 1981

I have been exaggerating my life. I have been grouping my whole life into one category, weight.

It seems so ridiculous now.

Unreal.

MAY 2, 1981

MY LIFE HAS BEEN ONE BIG TRADE OFF. I HAVE BEEN EATING INSTEAD OF LIVING!

I see now that my belief that other people didn't have trust in me was paranoid. It was a sign trying to tell me or show me that I wasn't trusting my own self.

MAY 4, 1981

I'm going to be okay,
not because I'm going to *make* myself be okay,
but because I'm going to *let* myself be okay.

9. Skipping Sessions

Viewpoint
I was a teenage Fresca freak

by Lisa Messinger

"Buuurrp!" The dead silence was broken by an incredibly picturesque belch. Every eye turned from its midterm to the culprit—me. I could hide neither the embarrassment on my face nor the Diet Pepsi on my breath—the secret was out. I felt like the words 'saccharine junkie' were written all over me.

It all started innocently enough. I had needed to pull an all-nighter, however my eyes weren't cooperating. Unwittingly, I swallowed my Vivarin tablet with a Diet Rite chaser. The pill wore off; the dietetic daze didn't. The next morning, I found myself craving Tab and Wheaties for breakfast.

My life became a relentless journey from soda machine to soda machine. I cashed in all of my paper money in order to support my habit. In a sac-

charin stupor, I sailed from the SAS basement to the Birnkrant lobby to the Student Union, where they have two. This eliminates the convulsions and epileptic-type attacks that can occur when there's only one machine and the dreaded "Out of Order" sign appears.

However, diet soda is only the beginning. It can lead to even more severe saccharin abuse. I needed the hard stuff. I began popping dietetic jelly beans between classes. Washing them down with Diet 7-Up was my biggest mistake. I woke up in a hospital emergency room having my stomach pumped.

By this time, however, my addiction was so strong I couldn't stop. I had to get "sweet" all the time, and the jelly beans weren't working anymore. Snorting dietetic gelatin became my

128

favorite, not to mention only, past-time. People started questioning my inflamed nostrils. Actually, this was only the residue from raspberry, my favorite flavor.

I realized I had a problem. However, I thought I was the only one. Phil Donahue saved my life. I saw him interviewing a reformed saccharin junkie. My habit could be kicked! That day, I made the most important phone call of my life.

"Hello, Sugar Substituters Anonymous, my name is Lisa M., and I'm an artificial sweetener abuser."

Since then, I've been abstinent. However, I still carry a few packets of Sweet 'n' Low in my purse—just in case.

Lisa Messinger is a freshman majoring in broadcast journalism.

MAY 8, 1981

Weight: 129½
Desired Weight: 120
Week One, May 8: 129½
Week Two, May 15:
Week Three, May 22:
Week Four, May 29:

Breakfast:
　1 egg
　1 wheat bread
　½ grapefruit

Snack:
　1 apple

Lunch: (Denny's)
　3 oz. hamburger
　1½ oz. white cheese
　Italian sauce
　1 slice french bread
　dinner salad (Thousand Island on the side)

Double Treat:
　1 family size "Chunky" candy bar
　1 family size raspberry filled candy bar
　1 single serving banana creme pie
　A little chocolate ice cream and a little chocolate cream pie

MAY 8, 1981

2:15 A.M.

I am looking in the mirror. Blob! Not fat. But not nice either. Rounded, expanded stomach. Jellylike, hanging boobs. Face that's quickly losing shape. Strangely shaped butt, like the muscles are in the wrong place. Thighs with a larger circumference. Same with upper arms. Hips curved. Waist wide. Not fat and not ugly, but certainly icky! I *feel* it all the time, this extra weight. Probably about 130 now. I want to feel healthy, vital and in tune with my body.

It's not affecting much but my body image, though. I still feel strong and good about other things.

But how we *feel* and how we look is something we have to deal with all the time. It's what we are.

Now, thank goodness, nothing else is wrapped up with my body and weight. So, it can go away without confusing me and setting me up.

Bye, bye.

MAY 8, 1981

3:00 A.M.

I don't like the way my body looks. I was going to say I don't like the way I look, but that's not all together true. I look heavier but not ugly, homely. I have a nice face. I like the way it looks better when it's thinner though.

I see now that eating nutritionally is not the only route. I could be (and was being these last six weeks) a haphazard, imbalanced eater. Whether or not I gained weight, I didn't feel guilty. However, I also didn't feel good! I got headaches, stomach aches, and even threw up. That was after I had a bacon quiche followed by almost a pint of chocolate chocolate chip ice cream. It seems these last weeks I've been trying to prove to myself that it's okay to eat anything I want. I'm talking *anything.* Candy everyday. Big family size bars. Fast food everyday. Everything I forbade myself before, and then ended up binging on. Now I'm just eating it everyday, whenever I want, without guilt, and without the purging of starvation the next days or excessive forced exercise. And, I've been gaining weight.

Now I'm beginning to see there is a reason to eat nutritiously, and it isn't to lose weight or torture yourself. It's to be healthy and feel healthy.

God, I've been through an emotional and physical wringer. It's very recent that I've thought thinness is only physical and doesn't really mean anything else.

I do have confidence in my intelligence. In myself. My basic attractiveness. My sense of humor. My writing. I'm a good friend. A nice, caring, empathetic person. Good worker, sensitive, ambitious, loving, loveable, sweet, special, wonderful, beautiful, normal person.

I know this *now*, and this doesn't change with physical changes.

MAY 10, 1981

Well, I don't want to be fat anymore. One hundred thirty-one! I'm going and that's all there is to it. I can't wait anymore. I have to do something now.

School. Well, I'll miss a midterm tomorrow and, what am I saying, I'll miss the rest of the semester. I can't think straight. I'm going.

Three weeks at this reducing spa in the country, $1000, which I have, and maybe I can get back to normal.

I just can't live with this kind of fat on me.

MAY 11, 1981

Dear Lisa,

Whatever you choose to do in life you will do well. I'm behind you all the way. I'm here whenever you need me.

I love you,
Mom

Dear Lisa,

You can take whatever suitcase you prefer. Hope you have a satisfying and enjoyable time at the Reducing Spa. We'll look forward to your call and seeing you when you get home. Hope you can make it for Liza M. and Joel G. at the Greek Theatre on the 30th. Maybe we can have a picnic dinner before the show.

Love,
Mom and Dad   (in Dad's handwriting)

MAY 23, 1981

I rebelled. I stopped exercising. I started eating whatever I wanted. Even though I wasn't doing any of my "classical" binging, I was eating a lot. I didn't like the way I looked and didn't want to wait until school got out or I could get off work. I felt desperate and I ran. I ran to the health spa resort praying to melt back into my old, tolerable body.

I'm still associating other things with being thin, strength and an ability to deal with people strongly. I see that happening when I picture myself thin. And now I'm not thin. I crawled back here after two days of a proposed three week stay to go back to school (but not to work right away) and hide in my dim one room apartment, phone unplugged, door locked. I haven't gone out, to a movie, to a restaurant, to a party since—I can't even remember when—because I feel fat and isolated and confused and locked in my own dungeon of a mind.

I felt that by running away, doing something so drastic and out of line, by leaving everything and everyone in midstream, it would be like slapping people in the face and saying, "I'm not what you thought," and then when I got back, I could tell the truth.

MAY 24, 1981

English Journal
5:45-6:00 P.M.

My university group therapy for eating disorders ended today. I felt it. Tears were in my eyes, but I also felt it inside. It wasn't as if I had been incredibly close to any one of them—Anita, Jane, Melissa, Jill, Heather or Kari—but, as Anita mentioned at the beginning, there was a closeness and a relationship within the group as a whole. I'm going to miss it, but I do feel that I won't close out the people in my life anymore. That group existed at a crucial time for me.

"Here Comes the Sun," that song is ringing in my ears. This is it, honey! You're coming out of a shell, a shell that was an incredibly cockeyed mind. So much has changed. You've discovered so much. Had so many insights. Learned a lot. There have been ups and downs. It can't be all up. Some wonderful things have happened. You've met some interesting, special people. One of them being yourself. It was a mishmash. Things hidden deep under the surface. I don't know where I am or where I'm going, and it actually feels okay.

10. Promises, Promises.

MAY 30, 1981

7:43 P.M.

As of June, 1981, I never binged again. My last binge consisted of an intermediate sausage pizza and an order of spaghetti al pesto. My stomach hurt and my head throbbed and then it dawned on me, once again, that I never had to binge again. I could control this. There is a difference now, though. Stopping binging is just that. Nothing more. This is, of course, the key.

Now if I can only find the door, let alone the lock.

JUNE 16, 1981

Sunday, 2:00 A.M.

WEIGHT: 140!!!!

I just started a fast. Obviously, that's the only way I'll get some results. No food will pass these lips. I am mad. I hate the state my life is in. Give it a week. Forget food. I'm not eating. Water, that's it. I want to drop at least ten pounds. Then, I'll see what to do. Fasting's okay. Other people do it. I really am absolutely disgusted, and it's time to *do* something. Really, *do* something. Nothing can make me eat.

I'll weigh myself Wednesday morning.

JUNE 18, 1981

I blew it! I can't fast. Therefore, I will go on the diet Dad promotes and *only* eat these foods in order to make this disgusting weight go away.

grapefruit
protein bread
low fat cottage cheese
carrots
celery
canned chicken
cucumbers
broccoli, string beans, green pepper
turkey

(With him walking around the house talking about it all the time—now that I moved home again—I can at least try it. Maybe it'll help.)

JUNE 19, 1981

Lisa,

Dear Daughter, we want you to know how proud we are that you can earn your living and go to school and take charge of your life. We have confidence in your common sense and ability to make good decisions. We're on YOUR side, no matter what. We love you so much because you are part of us, and nothing can ever change our feelings for you.

Love,
Mom

(I may have read it in the newspaper, but it could have been, and is, from me to you.)

JULY 1, 1981

KEEP THIS FOURTEEN DAY CHART OF YOUR WEIGHT LOSS
WHILE ON THE DIET:

First	Day 1	Day 2	Day 3	Day 4	Day 5	Day 6	Day 7
Week:	131	128	128	130½	129½	128½	

Second	Day 8	Day 9	Day 10	Day 11	Day 12	Day 13	Day 14
Week:							

Took Off _____ Pounds

JULY 13, 1981

Dear Lisa,

I know this letter is long overdue, but the most important letters I seem to put off because it takes too long to write down all my feelings. The not-so-personal letters are easier to write. Accept my apologies and get prepared for a long letter. Relax, have a soda and sit back!

I came home all ready to tell my family about my bulimarexia but chickened out. It seemed that there was never a time when everyone was together, and I lost my courage. I guess I still feel like I can lick this alone and don't need to burden them with more problems.

Actually, I'm hardly binging at all, maybe once a week. From four times a day that's quite a drop. I'm eating normal food, so maybe I don't need to binge and eat forbidden foods. I do throw up some of my meals if I feel I've eaten a tremendous amount. Overall, I'm doing better, and I'm feeling much better about myself. Things here have not gone well, but I'm reacting and showing my feelings and weaknesses instead of pigging out. Knowing that I can handle stressful situations and not fall apart has made me like myself so much more. Sure, there are times when I get so lonely or unhappy that I cry myself to sleep, but at least I'm not eating my blues away. I still have a long way to go, but maybe back at school with the group and a counselor I'll beat this totally.

I've been shopping a lot because it keeps me busy and out of the house. For once, I've actually been buying clothes instead of saying I'll wait until I lose weight. I've turned preppie and it's kind of fun!

Enough of me, how are you? Did you enjoy the spa? I would love to do that. How are you doing with your parents, especially your dad? Did you find an apartment or get housing from school? I haven't heard from Heather, have you? I really miss talking to you, Heather and the rest of the group. Nowhere else can I admit all my problems and still be understood.

For instance, I can't talk to anyone here about Jack. We broke up when I got home. I was furious at myself for not telling him to get lost because no one has the right to treat me the way that he has. Also, my stepmother and father are having problems again. My brothers were all very upset, and I tried to help them without taking all the guilt on myself. Things are better, but I still think it's a little tense. I'd like to go in for family counseling, but no one else seems to like the idea. So, I'm keeping a diary and trying to verbalize my feelings instead of clamming up.

Anyway, I'll be back in L.A. August 12, and during a break from moving in I'll call you. Hopefully we can get together before school starts. I can fix us lunch or dinner after I get settled, or maybe we can get together over a Tab! Thanks for the support!

Love,
Jane

JULY 22, 1981

Dear Jane,

I'm sitting here backstage on a talk show answering their phones. Fun, but not all that exciting. The perfect time to write a letter! So you'll understand if my writing gets a little messy (I'm writing on my lap), or if this letter seems a little disjointed (from people and/or phone interruptions).

Your letter was a relief. Really. I felt like I was reading something that I could have written. Finally, I thought, someone who understands, and who I understand! Over the summer I've been feeling like you have. Lonely. Unhappy. A little confused and angry. And everything's going pretty okay too.

Well, eatingwise, that is. Since I came back from the spa in Palm Springs (two months ago) I have not done any of my "classical" binges. I've pretty much eaten what I want. But, I got into the habit (ritual?) of eating whatever I wanted in the morning (pizza or whatever was in the house—but not binge-size portions, just single servings), and then I wouldn't eat during the day. I exercised, too, so I lost twelve of the twenty pounds I had gained. Since I wasn't depriving myself I thought I had normalized my eating. But I'm really not sure. One good thing is that I haven't been feeling guilty over these foods, but I haven't eaten them in front of anyone else either.

A couple of weeks ago this didn't seem nutritious enough, though. So, I went on the diet my dad was on but I was always hungry and didn't like it. For once I went off a diet without guilt. I've decided if I want to eat a big meal in the morning (usually meat and bread) then it will be more balanced eating fruit and vegetables during the day.

The amazing thing is that every time I "willed" myself to stop binging in the past, it didn't work. Now, it's just gone. And, as I'm writing, I realize why. I'm not being a perfectionist. For once! I'm just letting myself do what I want. I'm not "willing" weight loss either, and it's hard to do that when I'm not the weight I want to be. But, if I did "will" it, I know I'd gain instead of lose.

One thing I've realized, and it's been tough, is the value of real friends. I was lonely because I cut myself off from everyone for so long, and they didn't know why. Two good friends went back to the Midwest after school got out with me still not seeing them. I wrote them letters but was evasive. I didn't hear anything for a while, and I was depressed and mad at myself for being so destructive. Then, the day your letter came, Bob called from Wisconsin. I felt semi-uplifted. I feel, though, that I've made my relationships with everyone somewhat strained.

When I went back to work after my spa induced absence, no one had known where I was, or why, for those six weeks. I now feel funny with some people who had been friends. Even though I didn't stay at the spa, I still was given the hiatus from work.

Also, friends from high school that I had "cut out" are drifting back. Two girls, especially, and I feel so foolish for letting our friendships slide. Right now I feel like I'm rebuilding everything.

When you spoke about you and Jack, I felt like you were talking about me and Perry. Although I haven't admitted it, I feel very hurt. Since I told him "about myself" I saw him once in April! There have been extenuating circumstances, but I feel like he doesn't even care. I mean I told him I was sick and in pain and that I loved him, and from him I get nothing. Maybe it's just pride, because I felt only months ago that I was going to break it off with him. I feel like he's done it, and I wanted to be the one!

Which brings me to my next rejection story, Greg. We're both pages. We went out from July to April. I did nothing. He called and called and called. We talked a lot. We work together. I really liked him, although, at some points I thought our relationship was ridiculous. It was mainly platonic. I thought he kissed me because we started out that way. At one point I told him this. He said, no, that wasn't the way it was, and so we continued. I never understood our relationship. I wrote him a letter from Palm Springs reminding him how much I liked him and hinting when I'd be home. After nine months of calling, he didn't. When I went back to work I felt strange. Our first day together we got something to eat after work. When it was time to say good-bye he didn't kiss me. I felt awful and dejected. Not so much for this one incident, but what it implied. It was a blatant non-gesture. We haven't said anything, but I feel like I've been semi-dumped by two desirable guys I had for two years and nine months respectively. And no one even really dumped me.

Of course, I assumed both of them acted the way they did because of the way I looked. (Greg's standing here right now. In fact, he sat here for ten minutes asking me who I was writing to. I had an urge to kick him. I don't get him. He probably doesn't get me either. Talk about up-to-the minute letters.)

Anyway, another gray area involves my dad. On the surface everything's "peachy," but I find myself feeling very mad and frustrated about him. When I came back from Palm Springs, he blew up at me for no real reason. (A floor cleaning man rang our door bell and I slept through it. My brother did, too, but that, for some reason, was different.) He said he didn't like my attitude, or the type of person I'm becoming. He wanted to change me he said. He asked me how I thought *he* felt when he saw me ten to fifteen pounds heavier. So he was going to get skinny just to show me. Because of my "attitude"—which I felt was honesty for once, and felt good about—he said I couldn't use the charge card or go to the bulimia psychologist I've been seeing since February. This whole thing seemed unbelievable to me. Jane, I didn't even do anything. It shows how insensitive he was to my miserableness by cutting off my therapy, my one outlet. The ironic thing is that the reason I slept through the door bell is that I stayed up until 3:00 A.M. to jog around my pool so that I could weigh less in the morning. I've been doing this every night, and I've been tired every day, but of course I didn't tell my dad this.

(This guy just asked me to go waterskiing on Saturday. He said he's been wanting to ask me out for a long time but didn't. I gave him my number.)

Anyway, I'm getting barraged with phone calls. I wish I could write more because I want to ask all about you. So write and tell me. I can't wait to see you, although I can wait to go back to school. (I'm going to have to commute from home instead of live at the dorm.) Having you there will make it much, much more bearable. Take care.

Love,
Lisa

JULY 29, 1981

Lisa,

Well, it's about time I wrote this letter, How have you been? How is your work? I'm looking forward to coming back out to California in a few weeks and seeing you. I hope we can get together before school starts. My dad and I are driving out to L.A. We should arrive on the 24th and move into my apartment that afternoon. I'll call you at home that evening. If I can't get ahold of you, you know where I'll be.

Unfortunately I pulled a muscle in my calf while I was playing basketball. I'm going to be on crutches for a week, but I love all the attention I've been getting. My tennis game has improved since I got out of school. I hope I can go to two tournaments the last two weekends of the summer. I'll let you know how they turn out. I did win the singles league, and my friend and I came in second in mixed doubles. We should play some tennis before classes start.

I've been working about thirty hours a week this summer for that same engineering firm I worked for last summer. I'm ready to go back to school, though. After one year of engineering, working in an office seems easy.

I can't wait to see you. I miss you.

Love,
Bob

P.S. I hope you are coping with your problem. I'm glad to hear it's not that serious because I love you, and your friendship means a lot to me!

JULY 30, 1981

Dear Lisa,

I'm so glad my letter came at a good time for you. Yours came at a needy time too. You feel I know and understand you, and I feel the same way about you! Sometimes I can't believe how much alike we think.

I was happy to read how well you're doing with eating and losing weight. You're finally at a point where you can diet normally. I haven't gotten that far. I tried to go on a diet a few weeks ago, and within a day I was binging on "forbidden" foods. So, I stopped my diet plans and am doing better. I'm still eating a lot, but the guilt is fading. I really hate feeling this fat (I always do when I get up to 150 pounds), but I know if I try to starve or diet I'll only end up vomiting again. My first reaction to your thirteen pound weight loss was jealousy and the feeling that I should lose weight. But then I realized that I don't have to compete with anyone. I also realized how much you have had to learn before you could "diet." So now I'm truly happy for you and know that one day I'll reach that point too.

Your love life sounds exciting. You are too sensitive about your looks, especially if you keep getting asked out. You are beautiful outside and inside. Just keep remembering that. My love life, however, is not so smooth. Jack and I have not spoken at all since I wrote him from school. I know he won't call unless I do first, and I really don't want to call him. I'm happy without being around him all the time and realized how much I depended upon him for my self-esteem.

Lisa, about your dad, let me speak as the grad psych student I am. I think he's having a hard time adjusting to the new you. Before, you were the ideal daughter and weren't a threat. Now that he senses your changing, it may frighten him. I'm so relieved that you'll still be at school, even if you are going to have to live at home. You can come over to my apartment anytime between classes or to study or visit. Maybe we can arrange a time to go to the library together so you won't feel like you have nowhere to go.

About the family problems I mentioned in my last letter, I decided in the midst of all this that I could either take all the problems upon myself and go bananas, or I could love, support and be concerned but not let it get to me. I chose to not let the problems get to me. I will never be able to solve the problems we have, and it's time I started to look out for my welfare and stop living for everyone else. In a sense, it's like being conceited. It really is more like self-respect and self-love.

So I'm happy in spite of all that's been going on, something that's unusual for me.

Well, Lisa, it's almost my bedtime. Only one more day of getting up early. I can't wait to see you. Keep up the spirits. You're such an inspiration to me!

Love,
Jane

AUGUST 8, 1981

I have been reconfirmed. My faith in life has been renewed. I feel alive again. Much more so than before. Wherever this goes, I have gotten something important from it.

I've learned to trust my feelings. All the time I tried to deny them about this person and push them away, they were still there. I see that I can still have strong, potent feelings after these months of bulimia drought.

Right now, emotion and confusion fill my mind: I feel like I may be falling in love. The last time I felt that way with Perry it was true. This time, though, I'm a lot more confused. I'm just not sure. I've been pushing the feelings down for so long about this particular fellow page they're all mushed up.

Brent is . . . dynamic, sweet, sensitive, cute, handsome, intelligent, talented, funny, witty, going everywhere at once. I admire him, like him a lot, and may even . . .

He thinks I'm wonderful! Special, pretty, sweet. I really do feel terrific when I'm around him. It's not that he "makes" me feel that way. I actually "become" what he sees.

That's the nicest part. And I believe in him.

Maybe that's what love is.

AUGUST 10, 1981

After Francine had us "talk" to the food in my new summer bulimia group, I felt both a sense of strength and weakness, a feeling of exhilaration and anxiety. My first feelings were the positive ones. I had been so busy the past few weeks, that I really hadn't been as obsessed with my "progress." Talking to the food made me realize that I had changed positively without even forcing myself to. That's new because in the past I've felt as if I had to be controlling everything or else it wouldn't work. Here it was working without my conscious attention.

Those were my immediate feelings. The next day I started to question myself. "Where do you come off thinking that you're doing okay? Stop kidding yourself. You've just been too busy to eat." That day I was hot and tired and thought I was getting sick, and I overate. But without forcing myself to stop, I just did—without finishing what I had bought and for no reason except that I didn't like the way it was physically making me feel—and I just didn't want it.

Although I haven't been seeing Francine every week as of these last few months, going to her group twice a month is a good way to reflect on what's been happening (and a lot cheaper).

All in all talking to the food showed me that while I may have a grip on my problem, my grip may still be too tight. I've got to let myself breathe.

AUGUST 17, 1981

Well, Bob arrived early and what an arrival.

Friends for our whole freshman year. The closest of friends and nothing happens.

He's back one day and BOOM!

When he got up to close the door of his apartment after it had been open all day, and he came over to the couch and sat right next to me and looked at me, my heart almost stopped beating I got so scared.

This was after, for the first time, we talked about our prospective love lives. He's met Perry, but we've *never* talked about it. He started mentioning his girlfriend in Wisconsin. GIRLFRIEND! I saw one picture once in his apartment and then it was gone.

So, I told him about how Perry and I aren't really seeing each other anymore and mainly about Brent and David, a new person I had met at a work party who was sending me flowers and asking me out every weekend.

I told him how I was disappointed in what I'd seen in Brent. Here we were flirting friends for a year, thinking we'd be really good together, all the right components, and we finally "date" for a few weeks and . . . It was very easy for me to see quickly a relationship with Brent would not be for me. Talent, charisma, chutzpah, but what underneath? I couldn't find anything for me. When I wanted to talk it was like he had to keep it light and funny. *Had to.* I don't want that.

And then Bob, who has never sat this close to me, says, "What did you think of me all last year?''

"I guess I thought you weren't interested."

"Weren't interested? After you moved, you were never around. Never came around. I love you and I have for a long time."

That's what everyone had said. Noreen. Mom. Everyone who had seen us together said, "Don't you see the way he looks at you?" But I didn't.

And I said, "I love you too."

I thought of last year when I took him to the airport and we held hands to run to the terminal and I wished it were real. This Christmas I can kiss him goodbye, and I'll be his girlfriend, and I didn't even have to wait until Christmas either.

AUGUST 17, 1981

The urge to eat is so strong whenever I feel as though I've overeaten, even by a little. And yet, this is so illogical. If eating is the problem, then why eat to appease the problem? Maybe for a while I can't trust my body urges. They've been trained to work against me. Just because my body says, do this, do that, doesn't mean I have to listen. I'm tired of working against myself in the guise of working for myself. It's ridiculous. It's a circle that I get lost in. I get so concerned with staying on that fine line that *is* the circle. If I take a step in, I'll fall in. If I take a step out, I'll fall out. Or so I think. Maybe there's really land on both sides of the circle, and if I step off I'll realize I don't have to spend all that energy balancing.

AUGUST 20, 1981

From a page working deep inside a television soundstage:

Dear Perry,

I'm only writing because I'm so busy I'll probably be home for a total of two minutes in the next three days. This will probably reach you before I could even call. I tried to call you today from work, but you weren't home.

I've been thinking, I don't like the way we (I) left things after we talked the other night. You're right, I don't want you out of my life. We *are* friends. Finally, because I'm not exactly sure what we were

143

before. After we talked on the phone, I realized how far we've both come. We are different than we were, so how can we know how we feel? We can't. After I talked to you I thought, who can I talk to like this, this openly, about anything and everything, without being uncomfortable, even after not seeing each other for four months? This *is* special.

You're right. I was trying to tie everything up in a little package. And, of course, it can't be done. I did the same thing that I used to do: it had to be all or nothing. Which is ridiculous since I don't even know what "it all" is, let alone if I want it. What I see now is that I don't want nothing either.

I am your friend. I do want to see you. I don't want to cut you out of my life, and I'm glad that you don't want to cut me out of yours. So, instead of saying good-bye and good luck, I'll say, keep in touch.

Love,
Lisa

11. Love Affair

SEPTEMBER 20, 1981

I feel trapped. Now that I'm controlling my weight, it's okay to binge
again. I realize that this was the problem to begin with, binging as a
response to stress and other problems, and then watching very carefully what I ate (if anything) the following days. So, I feel like I'm getting trapped in that cycle again because for most of my life this cycle,
(not crucial weight gain,) has been my problem. Last year I binged and
didn't watch what I ate the following days, and I gained weight. Then,
this past summer, I didn't binge at all, and ate, to some extent normally, and lost most of the weight. Now that the weight is not so bad
(since I can leave the house and function socially, which I couldn't do
when I was ten pounds heavier) I've been binging and then regulating
again.

A few weeks ago, right before the first ''old time'' supermarket
candy-cookie-cake-binge, my mind was saying, this is going to be comfortable. It was yearning for that old soothed feeling. Those actions
and that feeling seemed a part of me, and, afterwards, it did seem like
the normal thing for me to have done. It gave me that comfortable,
soothed feeling.

I've also been binging when I feel I don't have control over my
time. ''Okay, so I've got to stay at school for hours between classes
since I have to live so far away, but I'm staying under protest.''
''Okay, so I've got to take this traffic and go home, where I'm not

sure I want to be, I'll do that under protest, too,'' which means eating.

Of course, I don't *have* to live at home, but I haven't even brought up moving. My parents said I could if I want to. I am punishing myself. Who should lay out money for someone who almost dropped out again, who runs away from apartments? I want to prove myself first.

I can see another part of this whole thing, too. I haven't been having any fun. I haven't been giving myself anything. The thing is I can't think of anything I would like to do or buy or give myself that would make me feel good, and I don't know why. I have been going out, but now it's with David, someone with whom there seems to be strings attached. He's so intense. Flowers. Cards. It's still something that I want to do, but it's not always fun. Since he's been out of school for two years and already works in the entertainment industry, he can't always relate to what I'm going through with school or my parents.

I can't help feeling that I am going out with him because Bob hurt me so much. I couldn't believe it. After so long, being so close, it comes down to this. The girl doesn't go to bed with me one-two-three, I drop her. Where is the sensitive person I've known, the one who said he loved me? Little did he know, because of the way I felt about him and feel, I was already planning a trip to the clinic. I was floating on a cloud. He stuck a pin in the way I'm looking at everything. I was ready, not one-two-three, but I was ready. With him.

Another part of what I've been feeling is that if I don't get it now, I won't get it, at least at my house. If there's cake or frozen pizza or corn chips, they won't last and they're not usually there. So I feel that I have to have it in the mornings. I don't have to leave for school at the crack of dawn. It is as though I'm giving myself something. This is my only do nothing but relax time when no one else is around, and I spend it eating and reading the newspaper or eating and watching television. I don't feel guilty anymore, I don't really care if my family knows I ate it, but I still wouldn't eat it in front of them.

I've been feeling the whole thing is abnormal. My mind is saying that the only way I could conceive of really having fun, enjoying my free time or enjoying most people, is to be thin. I can see it now. My mind is saying that although I weigh about 124 pounds I can't truly be happy without weighing 110 or 114 pounds. Another part of me is saying that I don't want to be happy just *because* of that. So I'm trapped in between and I'm eating. Then I think, what if I stopped binging and just ate normally and stayed where I am weightwise? I know I am just afraid, afraid that I'll see the way it should be and *relax* for once in my life and stop striving. I'm afraid of this, but I'm not sure why.

SEPTEMBER 23, 1981

I gained five pounds in the last two days. Monday, I weighed 122. Thursday, I weigh at least 127½.

Yesterday, I ate:
  2 little pizzas
  1 barrel of caramel corn with nuts
  1 bag of cheese popcorn
  1 bag of french candy peanuts
  2 hot dogs with mayonnaise
    1 in a tortilla
    1 in bread
  1 frozen pancake breakfast
  2 cans of coke

Tuesday, I ate:
  1 pancake frozen breakfast
  a lot of fritos
  2 pieces of fudge
  1 big cookie
  1 piece of fruitcake
Late at night:
  1 Jack-in-The-Box chicken sandwich
  1 large french fries
  And maybe more.

OCTOBER 17, 1981

Revelation 278:
I'm not weak because I decided to have dinner. I am stronger as a result of that somewhat balanced meal. Now, I have the energy to work on my essay.

Walk, walk, walk: that's all the students do here

By Lisa Messinger

During the first week of school I was rear-ended twice, side-swiped seven times; had three head-on collisions and was the victim of a hit and run accident.

But don't be fooled, I have a perfect driving record, and there's not a scratch or a dent on my car. Rather it's my body that's been scratched and dented not to mention bumped, bruised and mangled.

Lying in my recovery bed, I have come to the following conclusion: While it may not yet have been proven to cause cancer in laboratory rats, walking can definitely be hazardous to your health. At USC, that is.

Being a pedestrian is an experience unique unto itself. At first glance, it appears that the greatest perpetrators of the accidents I mentioned would be daydreaming bicyclists or tired tram drivers. Not true. Surprisingly, the gravest threat to our safety, not to mention sanity, is us. We've been stepping, trampling and stampeding all over each other.

Why? It's simple. We USC pedestrians are busy people. There aren't enough hours in a day to do our walking at one time and everything else we have to do at another time. Thus we combine the two. We walk and read. We walk and eat. We walk and talk. Boy, do we ever walk and talk.

Since walking can become habitual, rhythmic, automatic and even boring, it entices us to attempt more difficult tasks simultaneously.

Unfortunately, these other tasks drain concentration that is needed for walking. Just yesterday in the University Avenue/Tommy Trojan vicinity I noticed an example of this problem. A fraternity pledge engrossed in *Playboy* ran down a sorority pledge engrossed in *Playgirl*. While it could have been love at first sight, we'll probably never know since they were knocked unconscious and are now in comas at County-USC.

Seconds after the paramedics carried them away, another mishap occurred. A pre-med student who was trying to jog to class, eat a taco salad and dissect a frog all at the same time tripped and caused a 10-Trojan pile-up in front of VKC.

Clearly something must be done. I have an idea. But I'm afraid that to some the idea may seem too severe, too harsh. Nevertheless, sometimes drastic measures are called for: try watching where you are going.

Lisa Messinger is a freshman in broadcast journalism

148

Freeloader in pink boxers oversteps his bounds

By Lisa Messinger

There's a guy living in my apartment. He's not my boyfriend, husband, brother or friend. In fact, I know relatively nothing about him. What I do know is that he eats my food, copies my lecture notes, watches my TV, listens to my stereo, ties up my phone. And pays no rent.

You'd think he could be evicted, but unfortunately he can't. You see, he's not really a tenant. He's a freeloader, a pest and an annoyance. In other words, he's my roommate's boyfriend.

And until the other day, I was putting up with his little idiosyncrasies. That was until he overstepped the bounds of peaceful coexistence. First, he had the nerve to ask for his own keys. He wanted both a door key and a mail box key, since his mail is now being forwarded to our address.

Next, he asked if I would be kind enough to knock before entering the apartment. He said he was just being considerate since he knew it embarrassed me to find him watching TV in his underwear. Coincidentally, as he was making these requests, he was sprawled on the couch in nothing but a pair of pink polka dot boxer shorts. I thanked him for his consideration of my feelings and told him that pink was definitely his color.

Then I went into my own room to find his entomology project, a live termite collection, gnawing away at my bedpost. They had gotten out of their cigar box.

At that point, I would have given anything, even my pledge pin, if my roommate's boyfriend would have gotten out of our apartment.

It was then and there that I knew I had had enough. Being able to think of no other options, I went with the honest approach. I went out to the kitchen to find him at the freezer eyeing my Haagen Dazs ice cream. Quite simply, I told him to pack up his termites and never to show his spotted boxer shorts at my doorstep again. It worked. He and my roommate moved out that same night. They're now residing at his place.

Sorry, Arnold. (That's *his* roommate.)

Lisa Messinger is a freshman in broadcast journalism.

NOVEMBER 2, 1981

I did an experiment. I decided to live my life as an ordinary person. Average. Instead of above average. That's because although I am not ugly or fat, I don't feel pretty or thin either. I'm in between. I don't stand out in either direction anymore. I'm just there. Blah. Ick. Not awful. But nothing. Overreaction? Maybe. I can't tell.

It felt right to feel sick again over food. Like, welcome home. Comfortable. Like I've been away for a long time, but come back to the warmth, the numbness. Come back to where it doesn't hurt (on the surface) anymore. Come back. Come back. Come back.

NOVEMBER 3, 1981

Wheels are in motion. I feel alive again. I didn't even realize that I didn't before I left home to stay with Vicki since her mom was going out of town on a long business trip. But I can see now I was feeling lifeless. Honestly, whenever I'd eat, I'd feel justified because I couldn't think of anything else that was more desirable. Nothing. And I couldn't understand why. Talking with any friends, going out with David, it just took on no meaning. With everything I had, I felt as though I had nothing. That's when I began to feel depressed, and as I said, I couldn't understand why.

Now that I've recognized I was feeling that way I have some partial ideas as to why. I felt as though I was "doing," "putting out," and drawing nothing, no good feelings, from the people and things that made up my life.

I see now that risk is the only way you can really get in your corner the stuff you really want. Without it, you have to wait and wait and wait to be picked or chosen. Sometimes you're lucky. Those who pick and choose know what they want. Sometimes it's you, and sometimes, perhaps, you want them too, but not usually as much as they want you. They've gotten what they really wanted. You got picked. They got the thrill of winning. You get to feel like the trophy. Well, I see now I want the thrill for myself. Sure flattery is nice, but it wears off. I'll forego some of the flattery to do some of the picking.

That's why I felt such a rush from Brent and Bob. I didn't do it all, but I actively participated in the cultivation. I played a part in the desire process. Before I had them, I wanted each, consciously or subconsciously. That's the difference with David. He wants me, he loves me, he needs me, he picked me. I like him a great deal, but it's not the same thing. It's not the same rush, the same thrill of actively pursuing your life.

Now I've gotten that thrill with Greg. I had feelings and I expressed them. I don't understand all of them, but I know they're there. He is inexplicably attractive to me on the physical and personality level, and I wanted him to know it, and I wanted to know he knew it, to know that I counted.

NOVEMBER 12, 1981

No one has ever treated me as David does. He is so expressive. He is always telling me and showing me how he feels for me, making me feel special. And he's patient. He doesn't want me to do anything until I am ready.

I get to really, really like him more and more. I mean I liked him immediately. How many men do you see drinking Diet Pepsi at a party where everyone else is *drinking*? I had a feeling about him, and I was right. He had been heavy. Finally, I thought, maybe a man who will understand the desperation, loneliness, and insecurity I've been through.

And what do I get, a person never lonely or downtrodden, surrounded by *so many* friends. I have never met anyone with so many friends. He is so funny and outgoing and intelligent and has taken me under his wing.

We're becoming sidekicks, going everywhere together. It's not the kind of relationship I've gone for before, not that drop dead attraction (at least for me), but it's certainly the most comfortable I've ever felt with anyone. He makes me feel that way. I do believe he's madly in love with me, and that's awfully hard to resist.

NOVEMBER 14, 1981

Female wanted to take over housing contract in University housing as soon as possible. Call Penny: 743-2478

* * * * *

Well, I got it. My own dorm room. No sharing. One of the only singles available. I think I'll like it. I can be around people and still have my privacy.

DECEMBER 12, 1981

The murderess trapped inside the expanded and uglied corpse. Forced to live everyday inside the mind of the beautiful girl she killed. Remembering. Remembering what it was like to be beautiful. Feeling. Feeling what it is like to be ugly. Knowing. Knowing she killed someone at the utmost prime of her life. A girl who looked and felt wonderful. A girl who had everything going for her and was going everywhere with everyone at once. That girl is dead, but she was never buried. She's rotting inside of the murderess. Rotting away, but not going away.

Every time the murderess sees someone who looks like the dead girl, she hates them on sight and isn't always sure why. She hates them more when the boy who was attracted to the dead girl is attracted to the look-alike and treats her like she used to treat the dead girl.

She doesn't hate the boy, though, just the look-alike. She understands the boy. He likes a pretty girl.

It's strange that the murderess hates herself, but loves the dead girl. The dead girl was the only girl she ever loved. The dead girl knew how to be happy without trying, without force. She just was. The murderess can't ever be happy. She could die if she could bring the dead girl back. But the dead girl is gone. And the murderess is trapped.

DECEMBER 13, 1981

12:43 A.M. *IN A ROOM OF MY OWN*

I just lost my virginity to one David Sorrell whom I love. Unexpectedly and unplanned I let him come inside of me. He's madly in love with me. I wanted it like crazy. And now I don't have to climb the walls anymore.

1:32 A.M.
It's 1:32 A.M. and he just left.

Well, I lost my virginity while I was still a teenager. Just barely. A month and a half until I'm twenty. I lost it when I was nineteen. But there's still more to learn and more to come.

DECEMBER 18, 1981

Friday, 2:41 A.M.

I feel like I just lost my virginity again. This time there really was no doubt about what was going on.

This all happened after the ''Too Close For Comfort'' wrap party.

Funny, after the "Toni Tennille Show" party, just a year ago, I was happy with a few kisses. Not any more.

DECEMBER 22, 1981

When I walked into Dr. Francine Snyder's office a few weeks ago, I talked to her about my feelings regarding the murderess and the happy beautiful thin girl. As it turned out, that was one of the last visits I made to Francine's office, because that was the day both the murderess and the illusion of the beautiful happy dead girl died.

The vision of a murderess had been brewing in my mind for a long time, ever since I gradually started gaining back the weight I had lost in the summer of 1980, after my high school graduation. That was when for a few months I turned into the beautiful, happy, skinny, very popular girl I had always dreamed of being. It became etched in my mind with every pound that I gained that I was killing that girl, smothering her with chocolate syrup and malted milk balls.

Even through a year of bulimia counseling, although I have made incredible breakthroughs, I still clung to the idea of this beautiful happy thin girl who had proven to me that losing weight (as little as ten pounds) could in fact dramatically change your life. After all, I had been living proof of it!

What I finally realized that day in Dr. Snyder's office as she had me role-play the part of the beautiful happy thin dead girl was that I had not really been happy then. I had been a robot, a beautiful, popular, skinny *robot*. I neither really thought nor felt during that time. I merely performed robot-like actions. My life had not been filled with the happiness I now chose to believe it had been filled with. Instead, it was filled, and completely saturated with control, regimented diet, exercise, even dating schedules. I wasn't free, I was like a machine.

That day was the first time I cried in Dr. Snyder's office because I realized there was no murderess. There was just me, the same girl who had inhabited my body before I invented that robot, the pretty girl who relied more on her brains than her looks. This was not a personality that I had "visualized" and then "achieved." This was a personality that was just, somehow, inexplicably there, as it had been before the weight loss.

That day, I felt a wave of self-acceptance come over me that was different from any other such feeling I had experienced while in therapy. Within weeks I finally let myself fall into the love that had been building within me for David, who I'd already been seeing for almost four months. Also within weeks I was able to do something I had been ready and wanting to do for some time, open myself up and give myself fully to another human being.

It would be nice to say that ever since that office visit and the consequential falling in love and loss of virginity that I have been contented and balanced. Well, I haven't been; everything's been more or less the same. It's just that I've had another realization, another very important realization.

DECEMBER 25, 1981

Sweetheart, when it comes to Christmas presents,
You're just what I've always wanted!

Merry Christmas Sweetheart

I LOVE YOU
David

DECEMBER 30, 1981

Today:
   One "full" roast beef submarine sandwich
   One taco salad
   6 macaroon bars
   1 Carl's Jr. Superstar burger
   1 large french fries
   1 large onion rings
   1 medium chocolate shake
   Plus regular diet breakfast and lunch

JANUARY 3, 1981

Vacationing in Palm Springs in rented condo with family

I finally discovered that being happy is totally unrelated to weight or fluctuations of it, and I think it scared the hell out of me. After all, that's not the way I've been living for the past three or four or five years. It just crossed my mind a few minutes ago that I had been happy recently without the use of a scale.

My happy, elated sense of well-being really had nothing to do with weight or food. It had to do with feeling love and being loved and giving love and taking love. In other words, it had to do with being free. And this freedom of just "being" is so new to me. I liked it. I got scared. And then I ate again.

But then I thought (after eating and eating), why am I eating? Then I ate some more. I had gotten so used to having my feelings come through food. Now it still brings me down quickly if I overeat a lot. It's not so much the actual eating (as it had been before) as it is the weight I feel I'm gaining from it. The main change has been with the rest of my eating. I don't have to follow rules and restrict my eating in order to feel good. I don't have to be an exact, certain weight, to feel good. Recently, I've pretty much just felt good, for no apparent reason, and with no strings attached.

Then, the past few days I've been progressively making myself feel bad, tearing myself down. The strange thing was that it didn't start because I felt fat. I didn't feel fat. I felt good. I felt I looked good and not because of a scale number (I didn't know what it was), or because of eating too lightly (I wasn't restricting myself). I just felt good, I think, because I was letting myself be me and be free. I was doing for myself, and food and weight were not my main focus.

I was feeling nice without an incredible amount of trying, and now I'm feeling fat again. I feel like a seesaw, and that I can't trust or count on myself. Why would I want to take away an easy feeling of well-being to be miserable?

My eyes are tearing and my stomach is heaving because I had a sudden thought. Is it because then I am forced to go back into my old pattern? Yes. Yes. That's it. That's why today, especially, it seemed my interest was not in *what* I ate, but *that I keep eating.* Whenever my stomach could take anything. All day and night. I couldn't understand why I was doing that. It made me feel so much heavier that tomorrow I wanted to not eat anything—I felt boxed into that. Pushed back onto the roller coaster.

But why would I do this? I like it the other way. No, I *love* it the other way, and now I feel so far removed from that other feeling that I have to struggle my way back. Because, of course, I can't stay the way I feel now.

Later

I've discovered in the past few days that I like sex. I really like it. Maybe that's connected to the "stuffing" I've been doing. My feelings and actions in the past regarding sex have been pretty ambivalent. The past three weeks, the past few days, really, have been the first time I've ever truly let go, just feel and listen to my body. (I didn't even know my body could tell me such things.)

A couple days ago, though, was the first time, I think, that I thought, "This feels so good. This *is* fun."

The first time I was ever really involved in a kissing session—I was already over eighteen—Perry, my then boyfriend-to-be, pulled me back into his car (I was going to leave) and he said, "This is too much fun to stop." That struck me as very strange. Fun? No. No. No. This is serious business. It means things. It is something (I don't know what), but it is not (should not be) fun. I thought that through a year and a half of our relationship.

Then during this newer relationship with David, right from the beginning, I had a different attitude—an attitude that first said, you deserve this and then said, hey, this is okay. But I still couldn't just go with the flow. I still had to think and analyze and conjecture. I couldn't just be. And then I did just let myself go. Since then, I've just kind of been floating around. I've had the nicest, calmest, most serene feelings I've ever had.

For once, I just let myself be. I didn't make it a reward or a condition or make its happening depend on other things (like losing weight or something else) happening first. I just let it (no made it) happen to me. And felt it was the best thing I'd ever done.

So am I scared of this—this just being—instead of contriving or manipulating? I like it the other way, I want it the other way, but on days like today I feel like I'm screwing it up, and don't really understand why.

JANUARY 20, 1982

I started writing something, and I ripped it up. It started to take on a depressing tone, but that's not how I feel. Today (and that's all that matters) I feel good. There are no conscious reasons for it. What a relief, I don't have to *make* myself feel okay anymore.

My eyes are open wider. My mind is open wider. I have hope again. I'm moving in a positive direction as opposed to a negative one. Not being perfect. Just being.

I think when I started decaying is when I stopped everything else. I'll feel better if I exercise, go to work, go to classes, instead of not going because I'm not "up to it." I always get surprised and feel better when I *do*, when I live. I don't want to retreat into a shell and hide. Sometimes I feel that way, but it's not what I really want.

Things don't have to be *either* wonderful *or* awful anymore. There is an in between. I know because I'm in it right now, and it's so much easier than the *burden* of each extreme.

JANUARY 26, 1982

Dear Lisa,

I received your letter just the other day. To tell the truth, I was somewhat taken aback by it. Both by what you wrote and the way you wrote it. I feel that you must have changed a bit since we last spoke, and the change suits you well. Clearly, your life must be taking *definite* shape because your writing reflects a new confidence and assertiveness that I didn't recognize before.

More than that, your remarks about my letter were probably quite just. I wish I could read it again to see if I really did say things the way you said I did. You wield an accurate pen, but I won't turn this card into a rebuttal. What I really want to do is wish you a *Happy Birthday*, and say that I'm glad you want to get together. I hope that we will do so very soon. I sense that there is still much we have to say and learn from one another. The best way to do that is face to face.

> Love,
> *Perry*

FEBRUARY 1, 1982

Dear Perry,

What a nice card you sent me. I'm glad you want to get together. I had an idea about that. What about the end of February? It could mark the second anniversary of our first date. (Remember that?)

I'm glad you didn't use your card as a rebuttal. I had thought of that word, "rebuttal," before, while writing my letter. I thought, God, what is this, a debate or an argumentative essay? When I realized that's what it was turning into, I stopped because that's not what I had intended. You're right, if my letter seemed strong, I guess it does reflect a strength or assertiveness that's developed in me and enables me to stand up for myself.

You know, to be honest (which is what we said we'd be, right?) even though I was the one who said we shouldn't fool ourselves, I think we have been a little. I'm not sure how to put it, or what, in fact, it really is, but, whereas I can say to you, "Yes, let's be friends" (and I really want that to happen), I can't act that way. For instance, if I were dealing with another friend now who's ten minutes away, I'd call to make plans. Somehow that's not an easy thing to do in this situation. This is more complicated (feelingswise), but like you said, I'm sure it will be worth it.

I used to feel as if I had no basis or foundation to pull from—like a person fumbling around in the dark. I don't feel that way anymore. And I have to tell you it's one of the most freeing experiences I have had. Maybe you don't feel that way anymore either (or maybe I'm presuming too much to think that you ever felt that way, but I don't think so, and that happened to be one of the things I liked about you at the time).

Even if you do still feel that way, that's okay. People are entitled to be on different timetables or in different places. You know, that's so easy to see now, that we were never "in the same place at the same time." If we were, I (we probably) didn't know it. You know, I had you married before we even went out on a date. Did I ever tell you that I thought I wanted to marry you in eighth grade?! I thought, "I've found him." Tell me, who in eighth grade thinks these things? Then in ninth and tenth grade I had other crushes, but never one where I thought like that.

Oh, there's other newer stuff I want to tell you. I think I understand some of the ways you acted in relation to me that I never did before. You see, my friend, I think we're more alike than it might appear because put in a situation similar to yours I acted remarkably similarly. I was pursued by someone who was "so sure," "really sure" I was the *one*. Well, I liked him, a lot, but this quick seriousness petrified me. I wouldn't commit under any circumstances. I would make no commitments, take no risks. I can't think of them now, but I actually said things that you had said.

You know what it was, though, *fear* and way too much control over myself. Well, it's funny what's happened, I let down my guard, and let myself be natural. I'm not scared anymore, and I feel I've gained more real control (not the artificial control I had before).

I'm not trying to paint this as your picture. But I do think that what I used to think of as an incredible moralness and righteousness on your part was probably partly fear (for lack of a better word). Moralness and righteousness are, in my opinion, questionable as to whether they're assets or liabilities. Fear, on the other hand, is a perfectly human, endearing emotion.

Maybe through your newer relationship you've discovered some of the same things that I have. But I have to (or want to) mention a recent observation. Not to go into rebuttal, but at the end of your letter, you mentioned the girl you've been seeing, you said you were doing it so as not to be hypocritical about being honest and upfront (or perhaps, about leading me on?). Well, I didn't think about it until well after I sent my letter, but I wrote about David (my new person) because it was a big, nice, exciting thing that had happened to me. I started thinking that you didn't mention *at all* how you (or if you) felt about this girl. (Probably because you didn't think it appropriate, or most likely any of my business.) But anyway, I thought it was interesting that she was only brought up in relation to you and me. You said you were telling me so as not to "deceive" me. That's not something you tell to a friend. It's something you tell to a girlfriend. You're not deceiving a friend if you don't tell them about a girlfriend because the friend has no *vested* interest.

I hope you're not upset with my honesty. But I do live differently now. When I get confused, upset, or faced with misconceptions, I just don't bury it. I try and clear it up in my mind. Believe me (you may already know) it makes any important relationship better.

Believe it or not this started out to be a very short note. You're right, we probably do still have a lot to tell each other. But face to face?! I'm sure after all of this time, it'll be interesting, s-c-a-r-y, and very worthwhile.

I'm looking forward to hearing from you.

Love,
Lisa

(I decided it wasn't important enough any more to send.)

FEBRUARY 14, 1982

See Dick. Dick wants you to be *Happy* on Valentine's Day! Happy! Happy! See Jane. Jane wants you to have *fun* on Valentine's Day! Fun! Fun! See Spot. Spot wants to jump in your lap and nibble your ears. Arf. Arf. As for me, I think Spot has the right idea! You are the sexiest devil I ever knew. I love you very much.

All my love,
David.

* * * * *

When I'm calling you, you make my heart SING! Happy Valentine's Day.

Love,
David.

* * * * *

Happy Valentine's Day . . . to Someone who really knocks me out!

* * * * *

I'm a creature of habit! I think of you every five ~~minutes~~ seconds!

Love,
David.

FEBRUARY 22, 1982

And they said it wouldn't last! Happy six month anniversary.

Love,
David.

* * * * *

Congratulations. As always a brilliant performance. Six months and *All*-ways.

Love,
David.

* * * * *

160

Lisa,

These have been the best six months of my life. All because of you. I love you very much.

Love,
David.

MARCH 15, 1982

You get such a high because it's *you!* All you have. What else is there? What else is the point?

MAY 16, 1982

ON JUST MOVING HOME FOR SUMMER

Yesterday Dad and I took my car in to be fixed. We went out to breakfast. We played tennis. We drove to the store together. Today we played tennis again. Five sentences. Just five sentences. But, oh, what they imply.

We talked. Not just school. Not just money. In fact, rarely school, barely money. We actually had conversations that were a lot closer to interpersonal discussions. Damn close, in fact.

What's gone is the paranoia, the fear of judgment, the certainty of not measuring up. Or rather, the terror of appearing to measure up, but in reality not holding a candle to the image, the facade.

We're not all of a sudden soul mates, buddies, pals. But, then again there is that glimmer that says we two may be the most alike of us all.

In other words, all these years we've been fooled, or fools. Lisa looks like Mom. Lisa is like Mom. Lisa is Mom. Robert looks like Dad, but then again, not as much as Lisa looks like Mom. Robert has always been Rob, not a reflection, not a puddle.

Maybe looks are deceiving. I may look like Mom, but I'm beginning to see I'm a combination of both parents. I'm not like Mom. I'm not like Dad. I'm the indescribable essence that is both of them. Thus, I am unique.

Now that I have come to accept my uniqueness without malice as well as without exaggerated awe and glorification, I have reached a soothing, calming balance. Needless to say then, it is no longer chemicals or calories that sooth and calm me.

Being at peace like this has unlocked a little door somewhere on my body through which I have floated. For once, being able to get outside of myself. I slipped out, however, for more than some air and a little sightseeing. I broke out to join forces with my alter ego, my soul mate, my love. David is the acceptance, the support and the true know-you-inside-and-out-and-still-want-you-no-matter-what love that I never allowed myself to believe conceivable in the past.

That past, though, is becoming less and less of a burden to haul around. It lives on in the pages of this journal. It lives on, too, in a little corner of my mind. There's no rent control, though, in that particular corner. The rates for staying on keep getting higher and higher. Few of those old-timers can afford to pay, so they're packing up and moving out, leaving room for newer, more amiable tenants.

MAY 27, 1982

Yesterday, I saw a mother and son crossing the street. There was some traffic. Not a lot, but some. The mother went first not even watching the kid let alone holding his hand. Indifferent. Uncaring. Self-absorbed. Nevertheless, it was the only kid I've ever seen look for himself while crossing the street.

MAY 29, 1982

My last ''booger'' just fell out. You know, those booger scabs that had been filling, almost completely, my nostrils for months and months. I couldn't resist picking them out knowing there would again be blood, there would again be a scab. Over and over again the process, the cycle, was repeated. And now, finally, since I waited, hadn't thought about it for days and days, the last of the booger scabs has left. Naturally. Without my force. Just naturally.

JUNE 3, 1982

No matter what happens in my life, something must stay constant, a feeling of self-validation, the feeling of satisfaction with self. No matter what, this must *be.*

I've got to take care of myself. If I don't, who will? David will. My mom and dad will. That's the point, if I don't take over, keep charge, they will. And, unfortunately, they couldn't do half as good a job as I could.

JUNE 7, 1982

Oh, how things change. Everything in my life has changed, and amazingly I have not. I no longer change my personality to fit my mood. I don't feel like I'm a compound of different people anymore. I am just one person. I live. I breathe. I cope. I don't retreat. I don't escape. I don't muzzle myself.

JUNE 22, 1982

AFTER GETTING A VERY EXCITING RESPONSE FROM THE FIRST LITERARY AGENT I CONTACTED IN REGARD TO PUBLISHING THIS JOURNAL

I did that thing, that special thing, that I wanted to do while I was young, younger than would be expected of me. (Maybe it'll go, maybe it won't, but I still did it.)

JUNE 25, 1982

I've got a life.
Amazement. Wonder. Splendor. I've got a life. Not just the shell but the core.

JULY 6, 1982

If I could be thin, I could have a whole new life. The only trouble is that I don't want a whole new life anymore.

JULY 8, 1982

I want to be like I was even though I didn't like it when I was there.
Someday will I yearn to be as I am now, even though now, while

I'm here, I don't like my weight either?

JULY 8, 1982

You plan a whole life, but you can't even picture six years of waiting.
That's scary.

You thought, "I'm thinking marriage too soon." I could wait until
I'm twenty-eight. No, then David would be thirty-one. Too old. Me
twenty-seven. Him thirty. Hey, let's give the guy a break and shoot
for under thirty. Me twenty-six. Him twenty-nine. Good.

We can date each other and others, fool around with each other and
others for the time being. Then we could move in together one year
after I get out of college. Twenty-three and a half. And live together
for two and a half years. Marriage at twenty-six. Gives both of us
enough time to be (really) sure. And the folks enough time to save up
for the mega-wedding.

Lesson 281:
Don't discuss with your mother possibilities of future sex with as of
now unknown people. Even if you're indirect, she'll catch on.

Second Thought (Hot Flash via phone conversation):
You can't be all too sure about waiting when your heart feels like it's
melting into a warm, soft mush and you just want to lie down and be
hugged *by him.*

JULY 10, 1982

It would be so much less risky to playact with David. Make me so
much less vulnerable to playact it "cool." It's so much more of a
relief, though, not to have to.

JULY 13, 1982

I haven't been thin for a year and three months. And it hurts. It's
hurt.
   Current Weight: 137.

JULY 13, 1982

It really shocked me the other day to see Olivia Newton-John in shorts and think she has the greatest body and know mine could never be that fantastic. Then I realized that I had looked the same way in shorts once. After all, I'd worn a size three. I guess I'd forgotten or pushed it outside of my mind.

JULY 15, 1982

I'm not going to fall back into the isolation. I'm not going to cut myself off from My World. I'm not going to crawl back into my yellow wallpapered shell with the rose-colored trim. God, I'm getting beckoned again, though.

But do I have to go? Succumb? Retreat? No, No, No. No, No, No, No. In fact, No Way.

I can keep going, keep moving, keep the circulation going. I can listen to the directions from the cynic in me with one ear so that I can move with both feet in the opposite direction!

JULY 16, 1982

I know I've changed because I can get out of a "down" without going deeper. Before, when I'd start feeling depressed, that's what it was, a start of a who knows how long depression. Days? Weeks? Months? Periods of feeling bad that directly followed periods of feeling good. I can, and often did, look back on my life and vividly remember it in blocks of happy months or blocks of despairing months. No balance. No in between. Just a seesaw existence.

But now there's no more seesaw. I no longer spend all of my energy swinging up and down on a board that's going nowhere. I move. I may be unhappy, but I don't wallow and stagnate. It's not that I move because I tell, prod or force myself to, either. I don't need any telling, prodding or forcing. It just happens. This week, for example, I felt caught in a rut. Everything—David, job, family, education—fell flaw side up. However, maybe because I'm not cluttered and paralyzed with those subconscious demons anymore, my mind and body now actually have a natural, uninhibited response to such a situation, action. I worked out a whole course of study at school involving my first choice, marketable double major. All of a sudden my education seems worthwhile. I went to the newsroom asking about weekend internships and jobs. All of a sudden my page job seems worth holding onto. I initiated talks, discussions, fights with David. All of a sudden my precious gem of a David seems worth insuring. When this mood nose dive started, I thought, "Oh, no, could I fall into that pit again?" My question has been more than answered.

JULY 17, 1982

Another thing that helped me realize the nonconstructiveness of this and possible future down moods was my discussion with Anita Siegman, now in private practice, not at USC any longer.

I looked her up because I felt I still might need someone to talk to, and I didn't want to go back to Francine and have her think I was sliding backwards.

I asked her, "Will I ever be normal? Will I ever be like people who never worry about what they eat and stay trim?"

This had begun to worry me. Here I am, so much better than when I started out at the beginning of college, but it hit me that although my attitudes are very different, I still eat "good stuff" in private. Even though I feel pretty good at a weight higher than I would have accepted before, and even though I don't really binge anymore, I still think I use food sometimes.

"Will I ever be normal?"

Anita brought up a good point. She said I'm not sick. There is nothing wrong with me. Unfortunately, she said, we live in a society where this kind of concern for weight and body is virtually "normal." She said, "You know, you've lived this way for years. You can't just necessarily expect it to go away completely in a year or two."

Thinking about it this way has made me feel better.

SEPTEMBER 16, 1982

So, should I say I am living with David? Not officially. No name on the mailbox or answering machine (he says he doesn't want that yet). Not paying much at all. But I am here.

It really started when Dad said, "So, will you be home tonight?" For weeks I had been running past the kitchen when no one was looking with an overnight bag, then coming back in empty-handed and saying goodnight. Later I would call and say I was too tired to drive home, etc.

I was surprised at the question. He said, "Come on, you're an adult now, and David's working and out of school. We trust your judgment. We know it's a different world now."

So, then, gradually I started moving stuff in, and now I have half the closet. The nights I'd come back home he'd call and we'd talk, and we couldn't stand being apart. It was the most magnetic feeling I've felt for someone, drawn.

I have my own page friends, but I study a lot. He has so many friends and parties and I don't always want to go. This is causing some rift. He wants me to go with him, says he needs me for his career. But I have homework, and I don't like going. I feel so, as of yet, unaccomplished. I'm a junior in college (still at the end of my sophomore units), a little page, and these people are *big* in the entertainment field.

David says, you should be more confident, more sure of your specialness, and that these people want to hear what you have to say. "Don't worry," he says, "I'll teach you to work a room."

I don't know. I know I'm drawn to David. And now I'm a ninety percent of the time part of his apartment, the apartment I have always loved so much, and felt so at home at.

BBW
BIG
Beautiful
WOMAN

MAGAZINE FASHIONS FOR THE LARGE-SIZE WOMAN
Encino, CA 91316

November 29, 1982

Lisa Messinger
7089 Cardinal Drive
Woodland Hills, CA 91365

Dear Lisa,

Thank you for sending us your manuscript, "I was a Teenage Fresca Freak." We are always happy to receive and review articles.

BBW Magazine provides a national forum in which to expose writing talent. Many of our contributors have found being published in a national magazine to be a solid stepping stone into acquiring further freelance experience.

Please sign and return the enclosed release form.

Again, we appreciate your interest in BBW!

Very sincerely,

Frances G. Gazier
Managing Editor

Enc: 1
FGC/bg

DECEMBER 15, 1982

"A Gender History" Introduction (Women's Studies 210)

I dared to believe that I was different. I dared to believe that the world had changed. Now there is an emptiness inside of me because I see that nothing has changed and that I could become another obliging victim. I had dared to believe that I would be able to pursue a career to its utmost, cataclysmic limits and have a passionate, thriving, companionable marriage as well.

My boyfriend, however, the man I want to marry, a man who believes in me and all of my possibilities as well as believing in the rights of women, has told me that he doesn't see how this blend is possible. It's because of *my* chosen profession. It's because I'm going to be a broadcast journalist. He sees no way I could rise to the top (where I would like to be and he feels I should be) without spending "some time" on the East Coast. His chosen career, entertainment law, necessitates staying on the West Coast, and therein lies the rub.

We could work it out I said. We could have a bi-coastal marriage, a house in California and an apartment in New York and commute on weekends I said. That's not my idea of a marriage he said. I want to have you near me, not 3,000 miles away, he said.

I guess I thought that if you were going to be with someone for the next fifty years, a few years of stolen weekends and leading exciting, thriving lives wouldn't be out of the question. I guess I thought that finding the right person was more important than finding someone whose schedule was compatible to yours enabling them to be "near" you at all times. I guess I thought love was enough to work it out. I guess I was wrong.

First, I felt cheated because I am only twenty, and I'm already seeing possible limitations to a full and satisfying life. I'm already seeing that women still, to one degree or another, are asked to lead an "either or" existence. Later, I just started to feel crazy for even considering that such an alternative lifestyle was even possible or reasonable. Anyone I mentioned it to seemed to think it wasn't. Living away from your mate is no way to have a marriage. You're only asking for problems, especially in the fidelity department they all said. So, now I feel frustrated, crazy, selfish, and right all at the same time, a blend of feelings that I am sure countless women, present and past, have struggled with.

DECEMBER 17, 1982

I care about quality. I don't want my career to rest on ratings, a pretty smile, or the right time slot. That's not why I'm going into broadcast journalism. I'm studying broadcast journalism and women's studies at USC so that I can make poignant, pressing, probing documentaries about important social issues.

I have chosen documentaries because I want my career to be more than a three minute segment on the six o'clock news. I have more than that to say. I am a public speaker and a writer, a writer who wants to reveal, enlighten and amuse.

I see documentary making as one of my ultimate career goals. Your project sounds fascinating, the precise subject matter I am interested in. I would love to start my career journey as a member of your team!

JANUARY 11, 1983

Dear Ms. Aroza:

I have known since I was sixteen-years-old when I stepped into the KNXT newsroom as reporter Pete Pepper's ''shadow-for-a-day'' that broadcast journalism was the life for me. That's the sole reason I chose to come to USC—since it was one of the few schools offering a degree in broadcast journalism. I know the field requires more than just classroom experience, though. That's why I have been trying to lay a solid working foundation as well. Although I am just turning twenty-one, I have already been working at a TV station for two and a half years. At this point I am very eager to move into the television newsroom. I think your newscast is done excellently, and that KHJ has the best local talk show on television in ''Mid-Morning L.A.'' I would very much like to be associated with your station in the news intern position that is available.

I have included a copy of my resumé.

LISA MESSINGER
10769 Riverside Drive #204
North Hollywood CA 91607

KTLA, GOLDENWEST BROADCASTERS 8/81-Present
    SENIOR HEAD PAGE-GUEST RELATIONS SPOKESPERSON
    Supervise a page staff. Liaison between staff and eight
    television production companies, including: "Hour Magazine,"
    "The Richard Simmon's Show," "Too Close For Comfort," and
    "Solid Gold."
    Kevin Fortson, Guest Relations Coordinator

BIG BEAUTIFUL WOMAN MAGAZINE 12/82-Present
    FREELANCE REPORTER
    Submitted one humor piece, and have since been asked to
    write three articles involving interviews with a nationally
    known actress, doctor, and nurse. Articles to begin
    appearing nationally in May-June issue.

BARBOUR-LANGLEY PRODUCTIONS 12/82-1/83
    RESEARCH-PRODUCTION ASSISTANT on PBS Documentary
    Researched the psychological, sociological, and medical
    effects of cocaine and performed production duties on
    "Cocaine Blues," a one hour documentary currently in post-
    production.

KTLA, GOLDENWEST BROADCASTERS, TV PAGE, 6/80-8/81

USC BROADCAST JOURNALISM and WOMENS' STUDIES MAJOR ** 1980-Present
    3.8 GPA
    DEAN'S LIST: Spring 1981, Fall 1981, Spring 1982, Fall 1982
    Town and Gown Scholar
    Mary Nortrop Scholar
    DAILY TROJAN writer-contributer-humorist

CALABASAS HIGH SCHOOL 1976-1980
    4.0 GPA VALEDICTORIAN
    STATE SPEECH FINALIST, 1979, 1980
    CALABASAS CHRONICLE, EDITOR-IN-CHIEF

**Became Womens' Studies Major, 1/83.

JANUARY 25, 1983

Laura Aroza
Assignment Editor
KHJ News

Dear Ms. Aroza:

I really enjoyed meeting you the other day. Thank you for offering me
the news internship, especially since it didn't fit in with the UCLA intern's schedule. Believe it or not, however, since I spoke with you, I
interviewed and was chosen for a part-time job at KTLA where I've
been working for two and a half years. I will be the programming
assistant in the programming department. I will answer all viewer concerns and assist the program director and the two program managers,
and I am looking forward to it.

Thanks again for the offer, but I think I will stick with KTLA for
the time being.

Sincerely,
Lisa Messinger

JANUARY 26, 1983

What to do? Have I imagined this? What happened to the sweet man
I fell in love with who was *madly* in love with me and would do
anything for me?

Nothing I do seems to be right. He criticizes almost everything I
do. Maybe I am doing everything wrong. That's how he makes me
feel. I have to come out of my shell or I'll lose him, and our life, the
life that "will never be boring." If he leaves me alone, I'll be boring.
Why did he change? Or was he always like this and acted that way to
get me hooked?

I love David very much and I want to make him happy. I know
that I have certain personality deficiencies and parts that aren't
developed yet, but he can help me. I know he can.

And he's been my one confidante, the one person who knows
everything in the world about me, all my problems past and present.
And he's let me share his fun life. I think I probably should make
some or most of the changes he says I should. I'll try.

I just don't think I can party all the time, or even a half or a quarter or an eighth of the time. I'll just try and grin and bear it and be more open to it.

JANUARY 31, 1983

Dear Mr. Sorrell,

This is something I wanted to tell you when you were visiting from Chicago. In fact, I wanted to tell you before I even met you. I wanted to say thank you. Thank you because you have created the most wonderful combination of a person I could think of in David. I knew as I got to know him that he had to have some remarkable parents to have grown into the specialness that is him. Somewhere somebody taught him and showed him what it is to be a loving, caring, giving, warm, sensitive, sweet, beautiful person. All along, I knew it had to be you. Just the way David talks about you—you can tell that he is very happy when anyone compares you. And after meeting you I can see why.

I just wanted to say that I hope you are feeling better and thank you for creating a young man who is so easy to love.

Lisa

MARCH 14, 1983

no personality—wishy-washy—no opinions
unresponsive—insensitive
not friendly enough with people
don't *know how* to help him with his pain
    he can't tell me, I should just know he's in pain, just like he knows
    for me without words
put my pain on him, he can't be my psychoanalyst anymore, I talk
    too much about my problems—what about his?
I won't wear a bathing suit
I'm *dragging him down* like dead weight—he has to drag me to
    things.
I'll never do anything wrong. We have different priorities. Our values
    are different. Mine: scholarship, guilt. His: fun, parties
After eighteen months, not enough in common, like sports or politics
No stimulation.

No stimulating discussions for months
No emotional stimulation
I don't have it in me to change
He's been giving—doesn't feel he's gotten anywhere as much back.
    Can't give anymore.
He loves me. Will feel empty without me.
There's no future for us. He can't marry me, seeing the way I am.
Doesn't have patience to wait to see if I can change anymore.
    I wrote this all down so I don't just let go of it, go on and do
    nothing about it. With or without him I'm going to do something.

MARCH 15, 1983

1) Go see school counselor regarding my social problems.
        (She said I don't seem to have any problems.)

2) Join Sally's Figuretique ($49 for two years)
        I am going to lose ten pounds so I can wear a bathing suit this
        summer.

3) Sit and wait at David's

4) Tell him about 1 & 2. I am going to change.

MARCH 16, 1983

A.M.

Sit and wait at David's all day, but he doesn't come home.

P.M.

Tell him again he's wrong—I have it in me to change—that he's making this decision because his father is ill and he's upset.

    He said that's not the reason. We're just not right for each other, but maybe we can just cool it for awhile, not go out as exclusively. We'll call for dates, etc. That's when I knew I got him back.

MAY 8, 1983

Well, he died. His heart battered him and broke him down, and then just refused to tick. They gave each other a fight until the end.
David's father is dead, and there's nothing I can do about it. No way I can help him with his pain. Because he will not let me. He will barely speak. He sleeps and sleeps and sleeps. When he's awake, he wants to try and have fun and forget.

I can't forget. I cannot sleep it off. I can't forget his problems and I can't forget mine. What about the idiot who bashed into my car? What about the doctor who was treating me for my ankle and decided he'd heard so much about me from my aunt that he felt he knew me? What difference did it make that he was forty-five and married? No twenty-three year old guy could appreciate me, the brilliance behind my eyes he said.

He said it after the molest, though. When I think I'm getting examined and I'm really getting felt up (and then kissed) by a sick doctor with a waiting room full of googly-eyed patients, I call that molest. David calls it too trivial to think about. After all, his problem is much worse, but then he won't talk about that.

JULY 1, 1983

Moment upon moment I walk on eggshells.

I have it down to a science now.

Test question 1: "Will you go to the football game (that you hate) with us?"

"Why, yes, Sah. Of course, Sah."

There is no chance to say no now. Why rock the boat? If I say "No" now to anything, I don't know what'll happen.

I have learned to play the game. Finally. So well, in fact, he doesn't know I'm playing. He thinks this is really me now. I like to party now. I like to go out all the time. Hup. Hup. Keep moving. Who'd ever want to be alone?

He thinks this is really me. And now if I step out of character, he'll know the truth. And I'll have blown everything I've worked for.

AUGUST 20, 1983

Happy Birthday, David.

> *"Nothing yields more pleasure and content to the soul than when it finds that which it may love fervently, for to love and live beloved is the soul's paradise."*

I hope you like the cashmere sweater, it'll make you only that much more softer to hug.   *—William Bradford, 1630*

Love,
Lisa

SEPTEMBER 15, 1983

2:17 A.M.

If you love someone, let them go, if it was meant to be, they'll fly back to you.

David Sorrell
Lisa Messinger

    I don't feel the same need to hold on right now. I feel the only way it will work is if he *really* wants me. And I don't feel that I can "make" that happen. I don't feel, even, that if he doesn't feel it that I'm any less (of a person). Oddly enough, I'm left with the impression that he thinks more of me than I thought he did. So, I feel ahead. I have my own good impression of myself as well as his.

    I feel that I have no idea what might happen, but I do not now feel devastated or totally depleted. I feel like there's a lot in me. Not near enough, though, to change David. If he changes, *he* changes. I don't change him, and I don't change me to change him. That, of course, is what I was doing before. Now I'm calmer (?) because I know it can't be done.

    I believe I will be okay regardless of what becomes.

Later

This is good, whether for a period or forever, because it pushes, if not forces, me to decide what *I* really want to do with my life.

    Thank God I am not in a position where I feel I should not be,

176

someplace I went because of David. Thank God, even though that played heavily and I might be, probably would be, in a different place without him, thank God at this point I am at a place that feels right to me.

I actually, whether falsely or not, feel strong. Actually strong? Now that he's made the final break. I don't feel like I did the last time which, although I won't go into it, was a disaster. Hell on tears. Last time my initial reaction was to try and change myself to fit his mold. Now, somehow, I have gotten far from there. (I just pictured myself laughing tomorrow.) Not thinking about this every minute. Getting on. Without a cookie-cut future. Perhaps to write again.

Of course, I saw this, although not obvious. Turning off sad soap operas—dealing with death of the loved one—I cried and couldn't watch. I never cry over soap and death. Reaching out to David's friends, trying to pull him in (on the reel, like a fish) through them.

I need time to myself, or I'll be smothered. In a not right situation, I'll never know. It was, of course, too early or too late, or somewhere in the middle, but not the right time. I tear as I say, why don't we believe the people who say, timing is everything.

12. Real Life

NOVEMBER 9, 1983

I'm so glad I moved back to this university owned beautiful apart-
ment and lucked out and got such nice, wonderful roommates but . . .

Most good writing comes out of pain. Why is it that today I feel like
crying? Not yesterday or the day before, but today. Today I could
have just as easily have stayed in bed. Indeed, lay on the bed most of
the day. Soap opera. Soap opera. Shed a soapy tear. TV prompts it.
Real life put it there ready to spring from the aqueduct.

As I glance at the "I" that is written, I feel guilt. What's the use
of picking it all apart? Why, why be so concentrated on self? I haven't
been for a long time, and it's been good. Yea, baby, life's been good
to me. That's something you don't like to give up. It's hard to
understand why you have to.

I never really have put David on paper very much. Two years of
my life lived, but not on paper. That's what I did, I lived. Raw and
real, not self-conscious or hung up, but action, motion, lust and love
in the flesh. Part of me wants to say I love David so much and part
and part and part—I don't know. Here I am all by my lonesome, la,
la, la.

Here I am a normal person. With normal lusts and desires. I'm a
fucking normal person, and I feel connected with the world at large. I
can relate and understand and plug into those and that around me. I

am part of the human condition and I feel it.

I want to have sex. It's that plain and simple. Now that I have
floated to this spot that does not include dwelling on David, I want
others. Not just one, but several. Just for the physical. I want a lover.
Someone with whom I can be physical (often) and yet remain
myself—some distance—to be just me. Not a part of the bigger
something. Only me, with a lover. A young stud, attentive but not
smothering. And great in bed and to me. Later a real love and lover.
Right now I could truly get into some serious fucking.

(A part of me says I'm writing this way to shock compared to last
writings years ago. Part says, "Fuck, that's who I am now.")

DECEMBER 13, 1983

You realize the significance of the date, of course. I did, when I wrote
it. And before, thinking what I was doing two years ago, to date.

Fucking, that's what. Losing it for the first time. Coming the first
time and thinking, WOW, I thought nobody did that the first time.
Wow, what a great sex life I'm going to have. Ah, the grand expecta-
tion.

Not that it wasn't fulfilled. Just nowhere near wholly. Mainly, in
the end, I had a very good sex life because of myself. I learned how to
really do it well and was totally at ease with this man and he was very
at ease with me being the one to really go at it.

Now, re-evaluation is at mind. I haven't changed quite as much as I
might have thought. When it seemed that push was going to come to
shove, I thought long and quite hard about what I really wanted to do.
My body, very definitely, craved the touch in every cavern and space.
Every cavern and space wanted to be filled, longed for it. But then,
from somewhere inside all of those parental adolescent warnings
started talking, "What will you feel about it tomorrow? Don't you
want it to be with someone special?" Yes, yes, yes. I realized that the
same things mattered to me as had before. Yearnings, yes. Horniness,
hell, yes. But with anybody, anything male? No, thank you.

I'm still not jumping for joy. But I am okay. Everything and
nothing is up for grabs. The same old things are still the same old
things, and yet everything is different. I realize the good in my own
personal, very own, life. And I still have, somehow intact, every hope
for the future.

DECEMBER 18, 1983

The Lisa takes a lover. A lover. A lover. There are other ways to be happy that somehow come from within and through other people. Add one lover and blend well.

So the Lisa took a lover. A lover. A lover. Smouldering fires must eventually be extinguished or fed. Or both.

Nourishing myself is what I'm doing. I can see it at work. I am being nourished by the friendship and experience of the older (somewhat) women. Being nourished at home by the young spirit of the college co-eds I call wondrous to be around. Nourished by my family, my friends. For all the nourishing I did, only to end up malnourished and shockingly dehydrated.

Sperm enter me and nourish me. Nourish me. Nourish and flourish I will.

I am flourishing as an individual. And within that flourishing I can be nourished and cherished by those who surround me.

I'm (I am) glad.

DECEMBER 20, 1983

You know something, I just realized I still weigh 140 pounds. And around Thanksgiving I weighed around 143. And you know what, weight doesn't even matter to me anymore. I just eat what I want, when I want and that's it. I don't binge, ever. That is simply not a response anymore. I don't force myself not to, it just would be an unnatural action for me now. I also don't use food at all, because I know I can have whatever I want whenever I want it in front of whoever I want to.

JANUARY 8, 1984

You're on your own, kid. That's what crossed my mind in the bathroom. Funny, what crosses the mind in the bathroom. That was the first time I've really felt that way.

Something else that crossed my mind today. I am happy, and effortlessly so. I just happened to realize how happy I am and have been. It's just this thing I've been living in without really thinking about it.

And I realized that all of the things that made me realize I was happy had solely to do with me, stemmed just from me. The people who are helping make my life full now are my people. They don't belong to someone else and merely populate my life. They're my friends, my roommates, my family, my dates. My workmates. Wow, they really are all my people. What I was missing out on before! Taking seconds on someone else's picks.

My job (career) decisions. Actually decisions. My advances toward that special one of the opposite sex. I really am controlling my life. It's not just happening through someone else.

Ups and downs, downs and ups, yes. But mostly a calm, nice up. Everything, me, is just damn okay.

JANUARY 15, 1984

An interesting thought crossed my mind. I am proud of myself in a different way than before, in a way that says, I'm glad I made my life full and that I'm living and enjoying it.

Working in the television newsroom for the first time seems to be something to record for posterity. There will, of course, never be a first time again. I'm in, and that's about all there is to it. The news manager said after my second interview that I had more chutzpah than anyone he'd met. He said he thought, ''That girl has chutzpah, I'm going to find something for her.''

The old beau calls and the complications begin. Because no matter how wrong everyone now believes he is for you—you, of course, cared about him.

JANUARY 29, 1984

I can't think of what to write
because everything is just so okay.
I feel calm. I feel content.
I feel happy.
There's no man, no pinpoint
reason for this feeling of good.
There's a life, a lifestyle, being
lived by a fully functioning individual.
I can take care of myself.
What more could I ask for?
Now I can truly feel that no matter
what I have or don't have, I truly have
all I need, all I'll ever need.

Dear Josh,

Unfortunately, "Things That Go Creep In the Night" isn't creeping at the moment. It's one of the newest shows, and we've had print problems with it, and have not been able to air it as of yet. We probably won't be able to schedule it until May.

I'm sorry we couldn't have given you better news. I'd like to be able to get a dub for you, but I checked into it, and, unfortunately, I can't.

The only reason you get such special treatment, if you want to call it that, is because of your New York accent. I've been talking on these phones for almost a year now (I go to USC, write for a magazine, and work in the newsroom also), and you have to rank with the most interesting people I've spoken with.

Listen, I'm a **nice** Jewish girl, and I hope everything works out for you. Call if we can help you with anything else, or if you want to check on the status of the show, or if you want to brighten up a day otherwise filled with nowhere near as interesting viewer calls.

Good luck,

Lisa

Lisa Messinger
Programming Assistant

FROM THE CONCERNED PROGRAMMING STAFF:

QUESTIONNAIRE FOR MR. JOSH LEVINE UPON THE OCCASION OF HIS GOING OUT
WITH MS. LISA MESSINGER, LOVELY YOUNG THING WHO MUST NOT BE ABUSED.

1. How old are you, Mr. Levine?
   A. 20 years   B. 25 years   C. over 30   D. elderly

2. Why don't you have a car, Mr. Levine?
   A. Can't afford it   B. Couldn't pass the test
   C. I like to sponge off friends D. New Yorkers don't like cars

3. Which of the following TV shows have you appeared on?
   A. C.H.i.P.S.   B. Late-night Nudes   C. Gong Show

4. How do you think of Ms. Messinger -- you think she is...
   A. Wind, ready to be tamed   B. Innocent, like a lovely child
   C. Sassy, with a gypsy fire   D. Un Schickte Fleish Mit sve egen

5. As an actor, which of these things would you never do?
   A. Appear nude   B. Appear clothed   C. Appear intelligent
   D. Appear in front of an audience

6. You think of yourself as another...
   A. Marty Ingels   B. Tom Selleck   C. Mickey Mouse
   D. Gumby   E. No one -- I am unique

7. What is your most prized possession?
   A. My monogrammed underwear   B. My portrait portfolio
   C. My souvenir "Warriors" switchblade D. My letter from Lisa

8. If it comes to that, where will you and Lisa get married?
   A. On a romantic stretch of Malibu beach B. Married? You kidding?
   C. Anywhere she wants   D. A tacky Las Vegas chapel

THANK YOU VERY MUCH FOR YOUR COOPERATION IN THIS MATTER.

FEBRUARY 20, 1984

Hey there, ho there, hi there. Footloose and fancy-free and feeling fine.

Feeling like what it's like to really feel again. Maybe for a night, but maybe not and that's the thrill of it.

Feeling I've seen a bit and picked this one gem-type from the pool. Not the pool of life—but the pool of the months. Making him the most interesting of the interesting to bounce by.

Oh, la la. What bouncing this has had me doing.

It must be something when your life seemed the farthest thing from lonely, and then this person bounces in and it seems that if they're gone and not there you'll be a little lonely for them.

How come I didn't feel the least bit lonely til I met him and he's not here every minute?

What the hell has happened? One date and the girl's gone around the bend.

FEBRUARY 24, 1984

Even other women tell women to sit around and wait for a man to confirm their validity and desirability. Did he call yet? Why should he have to call?

If I know there's something to be interested in here, and every cell is telling me to do something about it—that I will feel good if I do: validated, confirmed, alive, vital, in control of my future—why shouldn't I?

I knew that I'd feel better if *I* did something rather than if I waited and he did something. The point was my taking responsibility for getting something to happen that I wanted. Why should I leave my fate—a fate that I definitely have an interest in—in someone else's hands?

It's not as though I didn't have encouragement. It's not as if he didn't say he wanted to go out with me again. He did say it and gave me every indication it was true. So, why the hell sit around and wait deciding that he was a rotten liar.

Why sully the real niceness of the evening by afterthoughts caused by the paranoid mind of a waiting helpless woman?

I felt good today because of what I did, not because of what he said. I don't need a man to make me feel all right about myself anymore. Since that feeling comes from me, I'm free do to anything I damn well please.

Catch up, everyone.

FEBRUARY 26, 1984

I weigh 130 pounds, and last night a man (special!) was telling me what a great body I have. Huggable, kissable, delicious. This is not something I want to record for posterity, but hey, thirteen pounds are gone and I don't feel like I really did a damn thing to lose them.

I'm a taster of life now. A participant. A liver.

I don't think I'm doing anything to prove anything to anyone. This is my life. I am young, and I want to live the way that seems most fulfilling to me. There are nowhere near as many no's as yes's these days.

I know who I am and what I want, and anything I do is not changing that. I'm proud of myself, not for blatantly external achievements but for the way I'm grappling with these personal issues.

FEBRUARY 28, 1984

Everything is so good and right and fun. I have so many friends and people that I like. I am in the newsroom learning, earning.

I love being with the funny, enchanting, especially cute actor from New York City who thinks I'm the best thing since sliced bread. But before him and during him and after him I still have what I had, full happiness and basic contentment.

I think back to a few—three—years ago when I'd probably only be writing so cheerfully because of my body realignment. Not now. My God, I didn't even try to lose weight. It's just that going to school in the morning, working four hours in the programing department in the afternoon, and working three nights in the newsroom left only time to eat for energy. My God, I didn't even *realize* until I stopped walking to school for winter break that that's what had firmed up my legs and hips, kept me from gaining weight, and made me feel generally *good.* Believe it or not, this weight did just fall off, and it had nothing to do with the main focus of my life.

Of course there must be some way things could be better, and things could certainly be worse, but I wouldn't trade places with anyone at all.

MARCH 13, 1984

David, I have a new lover now. He relishes my presence, my body. He tells me to hear him, that he is *making love* to me, nothing less. How can my eyes, brows, teeth and body, which he loves, be so pretty? He whispered that in my ear.

I think I took this thirty-year-old man by surprise ("Too young, too cute. No, sorry, an emerging woman, the best I ever had").

Who knows how long? Who cares? That's not the point. We're the point. We connect. We fit. We make love, no matter how different we are.

I feel totally free and myself. Not afraid or concerned with tomorrow much. Too occupied with tonight.

Give him to me, and let me make love to him, and then let me go my way alone tomorrow.

All my fortunes came true.

MARCH 18, 1984

How can I explain how I feel? It's all happened. It's all here, and it's all me and now. I like everything and everything likes me.

Lick that ice cream cone, not because it's going to melt, but because it tastes *so* good.

I did it. I'm happy. I have more people around me now. So many more people I need, but truly dependent on no one.

I really like sex. So why shouldn't I have it? I really want life. So why shouldn't I live it? I really like Josh. So why shouldn't I see him?

Yawn. Go to sleep. Happy.

There's a killer on the loose . . . grab a noose

By Lisa Messinger

Apparently there's a killer on the loose in our neighborhood, and he may have been aided and abetted by the Delta Tau Delta fraternity. If the story in the March 13th *Daily Trojan* is accurate, members of the fraternity helped a man who told them "he had just stabbed somebody and probably killed him."

Interestingly, this information was

tucked away in the 27th paragraph of a 32-paragraph article. Perhaps the reporter, like those involved, didn't see this behavior as unacceptable. How though, could it have been seen as anything but unacceptable?

Clearly, the fraternity members were in danger and should have acted accordingly. None of us would have expected them to endanger their lives and would have probably understood almost anything they had done to avoid being harmed. What they did do, however, seems highly questionable.

The DT said a man who was covered with blood entered the fraternity house. He was confronted by approximately 25 fraternity members. He told them he had been attacked by a gang of Mexicans. He said he had stabbed and probably killed someone, but as he was on parole, he didn't want the police to know about it.

While in the house, the article said, the man made a phone call and was given a pair of shorts by a fraternity member to replace his blood-stained sweatpants. Then, the article said, the fraternity members chased him from the house.

If these 25 young men were able to chase the man out of the house at that point, why was he able to make a phone call and given clothing beforehand? The article didn't mention anyone in the house calling the police. Couldn't at least one of the 25 have slipped away to make the call? Why, I think we should all ask, did the fraternity members react as they did?

Perhaps it had something to do with the kind of reasoning that was behind Theta Chi members summation of the situation. "He (the assailant) seemed innocent," _____ said. "He didn't seem like a ghetto person who wanted to kill anybody."

Well, according to the police and witnesses quoted in the article, apparently whatever man did want to kill somebody did so maliciously and violently, by not only shooting the man with a gun whose bullet grazed his head, but by going after the bleeding man and stabbing him to death.

Who, we should ask, put _____ or any other fraternity member in the position to judge and evaluate, or even contemplate, anyone's guilt or innocence? Now, no doubt due in part to that arrogant contemplation, there is a very good chance that a violent, wanted killer is roaming our streets or hiding out in our neighborhood.

Lisa Messinger is a senior in print journalism and the study of women and men in society.

MARCH 22, 1984

This will, of course, have to go down as the day I slept with two men within the scope of seven hours. Come home from one emergency room date, and end up in bed with your supposed platonic friend, who tends to be madly in love with you. Of course you were attracted to him, and on many an occasion wondered just when and if he would kiss you. The game's the same I guess. Goggly eyes and attraction. It's just that the stakes are higher now.

Well, I like Josh. And I like Chris. For completely different reasons.

And I guess that in part describes why I would have done this, and will probably continue doing it. At least with Chris. I keep swinging back and forth between my different ideal sex partner types. Here I am starting up again with a healthy perfectly built young man who knows nothing from clocks or time or nothing. All night long is how Lionel Ritchie puts it in the song I believe.

Do I sound crass? I don't know? I gave my heart. It was loved and cherished and chewed up and spit out. Why should I be jumping to give it again? In the first place, I haven't met anyone yet who I'd really want to give it to. I like staying in control, and I don't see why I have to stay in control alone until someone who I will fall in love with comes along. Right now high attraction in all areas seems enough. I like it. Why can't it be that simple? I knew with Chris it might not be, that we are not in the same place and he might want more. That stopped me for awhile, but in the long run I know you can't be responsible for another person. You can care, but you can't create their experiences for them. What you have is what you have, and hopefully it will be good for both of you.

It's very exciting and ultimately healthy, I think, not to know exactly where you're going. I just know I'll get there, not how.

MARCH 31 or APRIL 1, 1984

Well, what can I say except that I now know what great sex is. I know what it feels like to feel at one with another body. I know what it feels like not to have to move and yet to feel like you're floating on a cloud. There's no explaining why it's *so good* with this particular someone. It just is. It just feels so good. For so long.

I always thought that for it to be really good I had to move this way or that, really concentrate, participate, make it good for myself as much as they could have. Hey, hey, hey. Not so so so so. It feels so good.

Chris is so inexperienced and yet so perfect.

He says he loves me. I am wonderful, beautiful, ambitious—a girl he thought was quiet and studied a lot. Now he thinks I'm delectibly wild, and all that's good—a girl he wants for hours upon end.

It's funny what one stroke of the hand can lead to. It's all so delicious and warm and beautiful. I wonder if I can take a month and a half of it—until school gets out and he transfers—and all the rest of my months without him.

APRIL 4, 1984

Well, I finally made love on my own bed. Not in his apartment, or the other his apartment, or the extra bed in the other room. It's not a big deal, but it seemed the odds were against it. This has been my bed for over seven months and no one's shared it. Now he has, and I am a college girl in lust with a college boy, and even though that's not altogether true, it is. Sweet dreams.

APRIL 21, 1984

I feel elevated and airy. I know this is just a fling, and yet I know what utter delight is now. Just the physical. I've been mentally and mentally and mentally stimulated by rock managers and aspiring producer geniuses and entreprenuer-type architects.

Give me this bliss.

    For another week and a half.

        I can talk to my friends.

            Only he can make me fly right now.

APRIL 25, 1984

I haven't the energy after preparing eighteen units worth of final projects to think or walk or sleep, and yet I smile and am happy and am not annoyed or pained at the expulsion of my juice. Upstairs I find and leave in Ilyce, a friend among friends. What else could need filling? It's all there and within, waiting. Who could want more?

MAY 1, 1984

When you still remember the way David's robe felt, it hasn't been as long as you thought.

When you still remember the depth of the pockets, the little flicks of lint, it couldn't be that long.

When you remember getting out of his bed and putting on his robe and the way your body felt underneath, how could it have been that long?

It felt heavy like it was hanging on you, almost pulling you down.

Wondering if the newer one is wearing that robe makes you wonder just how long it's been.

And yet it's been quite awhile, you think, when you catch a glimpse in your closet of the black jumpsuit that jumped with him.

You didn't care then, and you don't care now, if she's in his robe because your jumpsuit and all your jeans and nice blouses have been wrinkled and smell like a wonderful actor who's about to return from a just long enough jaunt to the East Coast.

MAY 4, 1984

Well, he's transferring, and it's over as I knew it would be. As, really, I want it to be. He's transferring out of my life.

Chris is such a sweet boy. We have had a wonderful time. We both feel that way. This has been kind of dreamlike. Cocoonlike.

He says he loves me, is going to take the bus up from San Diego and visit me a lot. He does not see how different we are. He does not know that it would not work.

He will have to see. I think he already does. It will do us no good, and there is no use, in pretending. Although it would be dreamlike.

MAY 29, 1984

I don't take any shit anymore. All of a sudden it is identifiable and, therefore, avoidable or extractable.

Don't give her no shit, she won't take it. She doesn't eat shit anymore. She doesn't even want it in the same room anymore.
Jobs, even new jobs, are quitable.
People are leavable when they're shitdishers.
Shit's easily digestible when you can't see it.
When you see it, all of a sudden you don't want any part of it.
Why did I ever take it? And why won't I take it anymore?

JUNE 6, 1984

"You can't start a fire without a spark," sing it, Bruce, I'm listening now.

Just a spark these days. Burning. Flaring. Young and full of lust and love and adventure.

My body wants to be filled all the time. I'm young and fit from the

190

long walks and hungry, and full of a delicious actor.

Did I ever tell you that sex is great?

It truly is. Laugh and pooh-pooh at the past. This is it, baby. And there's so much more out there . . .

The artist as a young woman.

JULY 2, 1984

I want to be twenty-two forever.
Josh Levine has fallen in love with me.
Grreat.

Today I loved him being in love with me.
The actor not acting is superb.

Now is all. No more.
All's fine.
All's well.

Marie's my friend.

Tonight, my cup runneth over.

OXOXOXOX

JULY 7, 1984

1:24 A.M.

I do not just want to be young, old and die.

JULY 17, 1984

I do not want to need anybody. I don't want to cry and want and need.

He said he loves me and that took me in. I don't want to need.
How does it all work?
Where is everyone now that I'm at home from school again?
I've been crying a lot more lately.
I may have decided to leave it, but it still remains that ''News'' is all gone.

Everything You Always Wanted To Know About
Television News, But Were Afraid To Ask

"This is not a glamorous job," the manager of news operations told me as I sat stuck to the vinyl chair in his cubicle of an office in the newsroom at WDRT, a leading independent station in a major eastern city. As I took note of the large cardboard file boxes marked "resumés" stacked from floor to ceiling against the west wall of the room, I said I didn't want glamour, just an opportunity to work in a television newsroom.

Well, glamour was about as far from life at WDRT as was a forty share of ratings for their evening newscast. Whenever I think about those boxes of resumés, I can't help but wonder if those thousands of broadcasting, communications, and journalism graduates from Maine to South Carolina to Kansas knew how lucky they were to receive the standard WDRT "Sorry No Vacancy" letter. Would they be lucky enough, I wondered, to turn to real estate or paralegal work or perhaps managing a Kentucky Fried Chicken store?

I, needless to say, was not. I took the production assistant job that personnel hinted over 4000 people had applied for. It is my intention here to paint a picture of life in the television newsroom (I have a net-work of friends at other stations, who lead me to believe that, give or take a few ratings points, things are pretty much the same all over). It's a friendly warning to beginners, and a reference guide for all others who ever wondered what more there is to television news besides the color of Dan Rather's cardigan.

First of all, let's dispel a myth. Beginners do not really need a jour-nalism degree. This is just used as a tool to weed out the hundreds of thousands of other people who would apply for the jobs if the actual skills were really known. Let me, for perhaps the first time in print, set down the true prerequisites for most entry level broadcasting posi-tions.

1) Waitressing or waitering experience.
The production assistant or messenger or go-fer, or whatever the sta-tion chooses to call its hired servant, must be able to take dinner orders with the proficiency of a skilled, seasoned waiter. There is no

end, for example, to the variations on the theme of, let's say, a corned beef sandwich. There's, of course, your standard corned beef on rye with mustard. There is also, however, corned beef with mayo on whole wheat, corned beef on white toast with alfalfa sprouts, corned beef on Armenian bread with green peppers, and a personal favorite of one WDRT writer, Chinese corned beef chicken salad.

Although orders often come from such varied locales as McDonald's, Bernie's Vegetarian Garden, and Gustov's Goulash Palace, WDRT messengers are expected to do dinner runs in no more than twelve minutes. Once when an order of chicken paprika was held up at Gustov's because it was being specially deboned for our director Henny Sleinball, it took me sixteen minutes to get back to the station. Since two writers had already fallen face down onto their typewriters and the producer was forced to resort to cold Spaghettios from the WDRT vending machine, I was told to go straight to the corner and rip copy from the wire machines without my Big Mac dinner.

2) Professional race car driving experience.

This is on a par in importance with restaurant experience. Having driven in the Indianapolis 500 or at Daytona would certainly be something to list before *New York Times* or *Washington Post* stringer experience on your resumé. When WDRT couriers are hired they are given an official WDRT bumper sticker that says, ''Yes, that's right, I do own the whole damn road,'' and tips on such important things as how to easily spot highway patrolmen, and how to most effectively place your ''News Media'' placard on the dashboard for easy identification.

The correct placement of the ''News Media'' sign can become crucial at certain times. Take parking situations. When it becomes necessary to park on sidewalks, in hotel lobbies, or on top of other vehicles, it is important to have the sign properly displayed.

Couriers, on the other hand, do have some WDRT rules they must abide by. They are not under any circumstances allowed to drive over 120 miles per hour (it could hurt the car), and they are warned against driving through intersections while more than six pedestrians are crossing (lawsuits can be costly).

While professional race car driving and waitering experience is important job preparation for aspiring newsroom applicant's, there are certain academic prerequisites that should not be missed. Be sure to take the basic first aid or introductory pre-med class. This will come in handy on the many occasions you will get stabbed in the back. Make sure, also, that you read *Looking Out for Number One* and *How to be Your Own Best Friend.* It's just as important, too, not to miss the screening of "Three Faces of Eve" in the introductory cinema course. As most news beginners will tell you, this kind of knowledge is invaluable.

It's too bad that KiKi Carlyse, an aspiring WDRT anchor, didn't know her abc's when it came to backstabbing. She believed Carmine Rodanski, another aspiring anchor, when she told her a message had come in saying her grandmother had accidentally fallen out of a seven story building and broken her hip. KiKi rushed to the hospital, and Carmine, who was at that time an unpaid intern, valiantly took over her duties, telling Art Belchco, manager of news operations, that she thought it was about time he knew about KiKi's fiendish and uncontrollable cocaine habit.

As well as classes that should be taken, there are classes that it would be more helpful than not to miss. Do not, for example take anything based on Dale Carnegie's *How to Make Friends and Influence People,* avoid all communications classes, and do not take philosophy courses, especially logic or ethics.

It was harder, for example, for anyone at WDRT who had taken logic or ethics to understand why Marc Hereditarian was promoted than it was for people without these backgrounds. Marc came into the WDRT newsroom as a janitor. However, within two days, he was a six-figure-a-year WDRT golden-jacketed sportscaster. Later we found out that he was a friend of WDRT chairman of the board Carl Beefsky's lawyer's barber's son.

I shouldn't paint the newsroom experience, however, as such a completely harrowing one. I do think I remember that Melvin Bean, WDRT anchorman, did on one occasion thank me for my nightly carrying of his twenty-five pound full length mirror over to the news set. And if my memory serves me correctly, WDRT news executive producer Gordon Tinkle did once promise that if I ever worked six consecutive sixty hour weeks again, I might see a bonus in my paycheck

Lisa Messinger
Newsroom
4-4-4-4

of two Drive-In Monster Movie Marathon tickets for our local theatre.

Well, I never received that bonus. I walked out of the WDRT door that reads, ''If it's News, it's News to Us,'' for the last time about two months ago. I now work as a free lance writer during the day, and at night, in order to make ends meet, I work part time as a waitress at Gustov's Goulash Palace. As I debone chicken each night for the weary looking WDRT messenger, I think that what my new job lacks in glamour at least it makes up for in tips.

— — —

JULY 19, 1984

Twenty-two and a half inches. Do you believe it? Do you believe it? Twenty-two and a half inches—*TV Guide*, the most read publication in the nation, wrote twenty-two and a half inches on the copy of my article they returned. They inched out my article! This place that I wondered if they would even read my article, took the time to determine how much space my article would fill on the hallowed pages of *TV Guide*. It would have filled twenty-two and a half inches, I would have been paid, and it would have been read all over the country. Damn.

SEPTEMBER 7, 1984

I love finally knowing where things are in New York. It's hard to believe Marie and I were just in the city I had dreamed about so much. Now when I read and a place is mentioned, I can halfway picture it. I count out streets, I think uptown, midtown, downtown, the lower east side, the west side.

I see the city on film, in video, and I know it. I know the mystery now, but have I solved it? Will it take another trip, will it take more?

* * * * *

Four months 'til graduation is a short burp. Four months is enough to scare you out of your wits if you let the top off. Four months is enough. Four years, on the other hand, is beginning to seem like four months, just short of enough. Enough of a major independent TV station. Enough of a major metropolitan city, although I am a hummer, for sure, of "I Love L.A."

SEPTEMBER 8, 1984

I went into school knowing exactly what I wanted to do, wanting only to finally be able to do it. I come out of school not sure of what to choose, knowing only the sad truth, the utter reality, of a certain few dreams. Which are left? Which will do? Enough money, the right hours, but what of enough challenge, enough adventure, the eventual contribution? I never thought I would lose that desire, but I guess everybody says that. I still want to believe and hope that I may be different, that I am different. I'm just not sure anymore.

SEPTEMBER 10, 1984

Why am I so goddamned jealous of Marie? It's not that I'm really even jealous—envious, I mean—not really wishing that I was doing what she was doing, not wishing that I was making x-hundred dollars a week while still a student, not wishing that I was doing all kinds of exciting things in my chosen profession. Really, I'm not jealous. I'm just upset. This gnawing feeling tells me not to want to listen to my roommate's day at work, to the stories that last year used to make my mind perk.

She has money, and I don't. She has somehow leaped ahead of me. I was always ahead of everyone. Now there's someone so clearly ahead, and my roommate, my perhaps best friend. It's hard to live with such drive. I feel that I have drive, but it's on hold. It's hard to have drive and eighteen units and twenty hours of work all in the same week.

Like I said, I don't think I should be in that place now. I don't even want to be. I don't want to be on such a set path already. I like having dabbled, and dabbling in lots of related things. I write. I program. I newsed. I documentaried. I paged. I don't want to be pegged. But, somehow, because she's already working in broadcast journalism and seems so sure of exactly what she wants to do, I feel the pressure breathing down my neck. We're so comparable, and she's making money in a field where the pay is supposed to be dirt. She's pretty obviously going to make it.

Sometimes I don't even feel like I know where I'm going anymore. That's what I guess is so distressing. There seems like so many things I could do, and I feel terror at making the wrong choice, even though I know, at this early point, there aren't that many wrong choices.

Well, I have very important classes this last time, and I know I want to *be* there, not obsessed with tapes and resumés and all. I know this stuff is important, and it's the last time.

I know I still have every opportunity to be everything I ever thought I could be. I know I'm not even out of college yet. I know I'm a published author. I know if I had talent, I still have talent. I know that I'm not really behind, but in the right place for me. It's still easy, however, to feel threatened—aware at what seems like too many moments, just how human I am. Did I really used to be an angel?

How human do I have to be? Is this a test, or what? Really, I know I'm human. This is completely unnecessary. I don't need a pending romance between my roommate and Mr. Desirable flaunted in front of my face.

Why is he punching her? What's wrong with me, I'm not good enough to punch? Why does he have to be so handsome? So sharp? So built? Why does he have to live next door? Why does he have to punch my roommate?

Aren't I pretty? Does this mean that her personality so outweighs mine that it blocks it out? "Friendly" is her middle name, is it not? First and last, too. But that's my attraction to her also, so I can see it.

Of course, he's much more attractive to both of us because the picture holds three. He's not immediately my type, but are we in some kind of contest now? She's ahead, isn't she?

How did I always win before? Why can't I have whatever I want?

This is a test. I know it. Only a test of the emergency broadcast system. If this were a real emergency you would be told where to tune for news and information.

Viewpoint

Reaction

5 p.m., Sept. 18, 1984 — Boy, USC really has power, doesn't it? I just heard an *Associated Press* radiocast, a radiocast that goes all over the country. Most of this particular radiocast, however, consisted of chanting Trojans.

Of course, the top story of the day — the real subject of the radiocast — was Democratic presidential candidate Walter Mondale's one campaign stop in Los Angeles; his stop alongside Tommy Trojan on the USC campus.

The angle the reporter chose for this broadcast, however, was almost more interesting than the story itself. Not at all stressed in the 30-second report was the content of Mondale's speech. No, this particular report primarily focused on the audience.

"Reagan, Reagan, Reagan" — as chanted by various Trojans — was one of the few soundbites the reporter chose to use. Another was of Mondale telling the chanting Trojans that (Donald) Segretti was no longer on campus, and that they should be ashamed of themselves for trying to silence the Democrats. In his closing lines, the reporter spoke of "anti-Mondale," "pro-Reagan," and "booing."

Well, is USC happy? Are we happy that we shaped this report and countless others? We had an effect on the news that people all over the country rely on. We, at this all-important time for the candidates, may have very well have had an impact on the whole campaign. We can now say that we helped Walter Mondale get bad publicity and bad press.

Now, this would be one thing if it was accurate. What I question now that I am out of the humid heat of the rally itself, is just how accurate these reports will be.

Who were these hecklers? Did they really represent the attitude of the school, let alone the attitude of most of the people at the rally, or were they just loud? Rude? Obnoxious?

These people helped create national news. They may very well affect a presidential campaign—who were they?

If they were ardent Reagan supporters, that's one thing. However, if they were people more caught up in the fact that there were television cameras behind them and a presidential candidate in front of them, that's another.

As students sitting in that rally, did we realize the impact our actions and responses would have? Could we remove ourselves from the fact that we were at *our* school, in between *our* classes? Did we realize our significance? If we did, and we acted the way we did, that's one thing. However, if we were too nearsighted to see our own importance, that's a shame, and in the final analysis, may have helped to mislead the American public.

Lisa Messinger
Senior
Print Journalism
Study of Women and Men in Society

SEPTEMBER 22, 1984

Saturday Night

I am having an affair. The kind in the movies. And with an actor, by coincidence. I am writing a book, the kind that gets published, in fact.

He looks great in a towel. And I am delirious, in fact. Tell me, how did I get John Travolta and Sylvester Stallone in my bed?

In my bed. That's where we've been. In my bed.

Eight months. Peaking. Peaking, yes we are. An actor's in love with me. And I am peaking. All the while.

SEPTEMBER 25, 1984

All of a sudden it hits you, like when you realize you're in love with a friend you've known for a long time. All of sudden, there's passion, and fire, and you know what was so obvious all along, what was meant to be.

It was obvious, all the pieces were there, and you never saw what was right in front of you. The blank page. You're going to be a writer after all, aren't you?

SEPTEMBER 27, 1984

What happens when you might get a book published? It's hard to concentrate on anything except for the fact that your words might be
bound and pressed forever. Go to school? Ha! Ha! Sit still? Ha. The
infinite possibility that lies in the publisher's—no matter how
small—hand. To make you immortal, no matter how few know. Immortal, no matter how long it stays in print, because you would have
a copy to pass on. The dream. The dream of the writer.

But what of the fledgling? The unpublished? What of her? What excitement. The answer, the key. The start of her imminent, long-
awaited career.

What of her? Is it going to happen to her?

OCTOBER 1, 1984

12:30 A.M.

I fell in love. I didn't try, and I don't know how it happened. But I
guess it did. It doesn't matter where we go or what we do, it's eclec-
tic or electric or just wow! Everyone says that, but it's true.

I think I love him. Did he ask me if I'd ever thought of living in
New York? Yes. And I thought it at that moment. Us two in a loft,
an artist's studio, a little apartment. Writing. Acting. We said we'd
keep each other warm.

Just a thought. But I begin to like the sight of him more and more.
And certainly the feel. And definitely the sound. I'm a woman in love.
With all her options open.

OCTOBER 2, 1984

I'm walking around in a daze because it's not a dream anymore, it's
real. The thing that was just a dream a month ago is now beginning
to seem real. Plans are not dreams. Details are not dreams. Publishers
calls are not dreams. Talk of money is not a dream. This thing I
thought was my ultimate dream choice to do when I finished school is
now as real as anything else. Why is it that my dreams come true?

Epilogue

Well, clearly, it takes a long time for some dreams to come true. It takes a clear, unencumbered, uncluttered mind. It was only recently, really, before I realized that, although someday my journalism career might naturally bring me into the realm of broadcast journalism, that I did not have that "need" to be on camera, that I could be happy as a writer or print reporter. It was part of my old, shy, closed-up, insecure personality that had needed the attention and recognition that comes through television. Now, I just naturally have these things in my real life and don't "need" to seek them in a career.

I also don't need what I used to from my father. You'll notice he is not mentioned much in the last part of this journal. That's because, after the initial therapeutic explosion between us, I was already nineteen years old. Legally, an adult. When he started gradually to read about bulimia, see Francine Snyder on TV or hear her on radio and tell me about what he learned, I thought, "It's too late, buddy. You missed your chance. Here I am, I am grown up, and you lost me to another man, my all loving David."

Clearly, I was still hurt. However, when the all loving David broke off with me, devastated I went home many weekends to my parents. And I was surprised. I knew I'd get support from my mom. She'd call him every name in the book and be on my side. But, deep down, I thought my dad would think David was right, I should be left, I was not good enough to marry, I should try and get this intelligent, successful male back.

Well, at this very crucial point for me, I got sincere support and understanding and sympathy from my father. He felt that I was young and had everything going for me, and David wasn't right for me, and there was nothing at all wrong with me. He said, although maybe there was a sixty percent chance we would get back together, maybe we shouldn't.

At present, I wouldn't hesitate talking about anything at all with either of my parents. And I often do. My mom always understands. My dad many times does. I am now, however, more than aware that he cares about me, all parts of me, not just the brain and the outer crust.

Also, you might note, there's little mention in the last part of the journal of food or weight or body measurements. I don't think about it anymore. I don't have to tell you how it happened. You have seen what a long, complex process was involved. I have to say, as I sit in front of my buzzing typewriter that is working on newspaper deadline time, that my dream really did come true. When I went in to Anita Siegman's office three years ago, after a whole year and a half of recovery, I asked her if I would ever be normal, would ever be like those thin people who stay their normal weight and do not think or worry or calculate about food. She said, "Don't worry. You're fine now. Many people in society live as you are right now, and it takes time."

Well, that soothed me and helped me to keep plugging along. What I realized, though, about a year later—fully two and a half years after I first saw Dr. Francine Snyder—was that, without realizing it, I had crossed over the line. I had crossed over the line and become completely free as a person and a woman. That was two years ago.

Needless to say, although there is pressure to do so in our current society, women do not need to be slaves to their bodies or their scales. Just walk away! It may be a long walk but that will only make your legs all the more strong.

November, 1985

Afterword

Lisa Messinger has referred to bulimia as a murder of the self. Yet, it took her many years and much inner turmoil to understand that her dis-ease was actually the enactment of a ritual murder, not of her 'fat' self, not of her 'thin' self, but of her 'true' self, her self as a woman writer.

I see Lisa Messinger's bulimarexia journal as a "rite de passage," a mythic rite that many women in our culture today engage in, women who are desperately seeking some form of legitimation (read here also some kind of "blessing") that will enable them to develop those larger, grander, more monumental aspects of the 'self' that nurture their creative spirit.

Ours is a patriarchal culture with almost no empowering images for women. Devoid of a female image of the cosmic creator (we have no goddesses in the Judeo-Christian tradition), women artists must struggle to give birth to the vaster dimensions of the female self in a world that teaches them that women will only receive love by diminishing themselves. They learn that it is through self-deprivation and self-sacrifice that they will be rewarded, not through empowerment or creation. Starvation today is literally killing not only the bodies, but also the minds of many modern American women. Our culture's reduction of women to a minimum on all levels is manifesting itself in a nationwide epidemic of bulimia and anorexia in today's college population. I understand this crisis as the exterior form of a much more dangerous reduction of women on a very deep, psychic level. As paradoxical as it may seem, America, the richest country in the world, has a new population of both poor and starving women.

How can women be encouraged to pursue high achievement, to give birth to new cultural forms, or to climb the mythical ladder of success that the media presents to them (as if it existed in a non-sexist, egalitarian world) when they are simultaneously being socialized to realize only the most diminitive, reduced versions of their full human potential?

It seems to me that bulimarexia is the living symbol of the dilemma of modern woman struggling to reconcile the greater aspects of her creative self with society's reductionistic portrait of her ''feminine'' nature as it has been traditionally rendered. It is not because Lisa Messinger aspired at one point to be a broadcast journalist that she has evaded our culture's programming of the minimalization and trivialization of women. In the mentality of typical media double-think, the image that we broadcast creates the illusion of reality. Thus, if a woman looks diminutive, she might not be seen for what she really is—an ambitious, aspiring and successful intellectual creator. Since the role of creator has traditionally been ascribed to the male in our culture, were she to openly present herself in the image of creator, she might run the risk of being perceived as a threatening female.

It has been said that if there is a female aesthetic (a topic which is still hotly debated), it is based upon the form of the patchwork, the grid, the quilt, or the diary. Because women's time has historically been punctuated by a series of constant interruptions, by the intrusion of their personal domestic responsibilities upon their creative lives, (cooking, cleaning, shopping, caring for the children, etc.) women tend to create in small discrete segments. The diary form certainly ex- emplifies this model. Yet, the diary also permits us, at last, to consider the personal subject matter of a woman's life as suitable and serious enough for art. It transforms what once might have been considered to be merely trivial into a matter of central importance.

Within the flexibility of the genre of the journal, Lisa has, never- theless, crafted an artistic form; she has created a composition which progresses steadily in a rhythmic crescendo to an artistic resolution. Her form includes other kinds of documents as well, all of which create their own subtexts within the work. These letters from boyfriends, girlfriends, and relatives, these lists of foods eaten, calories consumed, and the progressive physical measurements and weight charts literally extend the resonance of the events in her life and point the way to larger metaphoric meanings. Perhaps the most interesting of these items is the collection of Lisa's articles written for the university newspaper, for they tell another tale of liberation from conventional norms, a tale that parallels her liberation from bulimia, and traces the development of her self-consciousness as a writer. The earliest of these articles is coy, ironic, sophomoric, and conventional humorous. The last articles, however, are deeply felt editorial comments. Thus, the journal documents Lisa's intellectual maturation through the evolution of her efforts to find a voice as she grows in strength as a writer and a thinker.

The publication of this journal intact preserves the integrity of a life that is *not fictional* but *real*. And one of the more important themes of her real life was Abstention. The many pages which just bear a date and nothing more attest to the impact of the ethnic of Abstention upon her. The concretization of the aesthetic of the minimal female self, both in terms of her weight and in terms of the actual length of her diary entries is extremely poignant. The literal overcoming of her bulimia is literary as well, as is attested to in the final expansion of her journal entries. The permission she has given herself to eat naturally, to nurture herself on the physical level corresponds to the permission she has also given herself to express herself more fully. To develop her mind and her writing simultaneously.

Lisa Messinger's journal is more than just the journal of any woman who has suffered from bulimia. It is the journal of a very specific woman, a talented writer. In fact, it is the dramatic proof of how a woman's creativity can flourish in an environment that permits her to nourish herself, not only physically, but mentally, emotionally, and spiritually as well. It is my fervent wish that as this journal touches other young women who have suffered from this problem, they, too, will seek to develop the larger parts of themselves that have been starved and stifled by a society which tells them that only the most diminished aspects of women are valuable.

For those other women, then, and for their parents, friends, relatives, and teachers who will read this book hoping to learn something about how they can help someone suffering from bulimia, it is important to read the life of the woman writer as a metaphor for the life of the supressed creativity of any woman that is being malnourished in our culture.

Lisa's journal ends in recovery, the recovery of her artistic self. If her journal can help other women to find a way out of their compulsive obsessions to reduce themselves, we can certainly look forward to a future generation of dynamic, empowered and creative young women. These are the women whose histories have been written out of our heritage. These are the women who will, hopefully, lead our civilization into an era of balance in which the "feminine" (understood not as a stereotype, but as a powerful energy) will no longer be erased from the human record.

The journey to recovery for women of today is then made possible through the healing process of creation. Since the diary was written, Lisa has taken her place in the professional world of journalism. She is a fine writer, and we all await her future works with enthusiasm, encouragement, and pride.

Gloria Orenstein
Associate Professor of Comparative
Literature and the Program for the Study
of Women and Men in Society at the
University of Southern California.
October 1985